How FAR IS TOO FAR

HOW FAR IS TOO FAR

How FAR IS TOO FAR?

HOW FAR IS TOO FAR?

FAR IS TOO FAR?

WHERE TO DRAW THE LINE ON PREMARITAL
SEX & PHYSICAL INTIMACY

TODD LOCHNER
WITH DOUG HALEY AND CHRIS PIPER

BROWN BOOKS PUBLISHING GROUP
DALLAS, TEXAS

HOW FAR IS TOO FAR?

© 2004 Todd Lochner

For information, please contact
Brown Books Publishing Group
16200 North Dallas Parkway, Suite 170
Dallas, Texas 75248
www.brownbooks.com

ISBN 0-9753907-2-4
LCCN 2004110053
First Printing, 2004

Contents

Acknowledgments

Jesus Christ: For your amazing love. There is nothing greater!

When I was asked to write a book in order to share my message regarding premarital sex and physical intimacy, I was literally scared to death. It's easy to get up and share something with a microphone in your hand, but to capture that emotion in print is the most challenging thing I have done in years. It's hard enough just to get me to read a book, much less write one. This has been an amazing journey in which I have learned so much. The most important thing I learned is that when God has a message He wants heard, nothing will get in His way! I would like to thank some very special people who enabled me to see the light at the end of the tunnel.

Stacy: For staying by my side and encouraging me to finish. You're an amazing woman! It just goes to show that God can and does bless his children way beyond their imaginations. I am living proof that you can marry way out of your league. Thanks for loving me.

Mom: For never allowing me to forget how much Jesus loves me. The Christian foundation you provided was like an incredible road map that always showed me the way home when I got off course. I love you.

Doug Haley: For believing in this project wholeheartedly! Thanks for your help and support!

Chris Piper: For your enthusiasm! If it were not for your excitement and belief in this book, I probably would not have completed the project. You pushed me beyond my own potential. God used you in a powerful way. It is so incredible to see a college student with so much talent "sold-out" for Jesus Christ.

Don Piper: For hearing and following God's calling in your life to serve HIM. You have impacted lives more than you will ever know. You were a dad when I needed one the most. You are the ultimate mentor. Thanks for always being there!

Robbie Robison: For being a true friend and the best bud a guy could have. You rock!

Greg Perry: For believing in me and always providing encouragement when I needed it the most. You are a true brother in Christ.

David Russell: For your support and donating so much of your talent and time.

Richard Ross: For your initial challenge to put my message in print.

9th Grade Guys—Valley Creek Church: For asking me every Sunday, "How's the book coming—is it finished yet?" You guys will never know how much that helped me stay on track. Thanks for holding me accountable. You're the best!

Brown Books: For believing in this project and making it a reality.

And finally, for you, **The Reader:** For choosing this book! I pray that you will open your mind and soften your heart to the message you are about to read. God bless you.

Foreword

How Far Is Too Far? **is a preemptive strike in the area of runaway human sexuality as expressed by folks not nearly ready to experience it.**

I was barely out of adolescence myself as a fledgling student minister when I had my first encounter with a teen in real trouble. A soft-spoken young lady whose parents were the ubiquitous "pillars of the church," asked me if she could talk to me for a minute—even though her friends presently surrounded us, I sensed her urgency.

"Sure," I offered.

We went around the corner to my office and she sat down. I tried to make small talk but she was in no mood. After a couple of awkward moments I finally asked, "Did you have something you wanted to tell me?" "Uh–huh," she meekly muttered, lowering her head, "I think I'm pregnant."

Fifteen years of age and on her way to parenthood. That would be the first of far too many encounters where young boys and girls would give me gut-wrenching news of pregnancies, STDs, broken hearts, and families in crisis. It's a legacy I have experienced repeatedly, as late as this very year.

Are we humans helpless, ignorant, or just plain stupid? Since the Garden of Eden, have we not yet found a way to control our passions and find authentic love?

Todd Lochner has written a powerful book for teens, young adults, and those who care for them. He tackles the age-old question: "How Far Is Too Far?" From adolescents who really are hormones on two legs, to young single adults looking for love in all the wrong places, Todd pulls no punches. Yet his experience and advice are thoughtful and redemptive.

I have mentored Todd from the time he was just a puppy until full-blown, responsible manhood. We have shared delirious joyful moments and times of great sadness and bitter tears. In one of life's interesting turnabouts, Todd became the son who adopted a father and that father was me. It hasn't always been easy, but I couldn't be more proud of him. Against all odds and through the amazing forbearance of God the Father, Todd has overcome. Through his own painful and sometimes tragic past, Todd Lochner now courageously prepares people of all ages to face their weaknesses and provides an amazing game plan for inevitable temptations.

If there is one crucial thing I have learned from those who came before me it is this: You must decide IN ADVANCE of any temptation how you will handle it when it comes—for it WILL come.

As Todd would say, he's a person who shoots straight. You'll find no varnish or candy-coating here. What you will find is a young man with boundless talent and the worst case of potential I've ever encountered, who got his life together and is making a difference in the lives of others.

It's not a "Do-As-I-Say" book. Quite the contrary—it's in your face! It's practical. It's doable. It will work in the lives of teens, singles, or anyone struggling with the question: "How Far Is Too Far?"

So fasten your seatbelts . . . Here are the answers you've been looking for, from a young man who found out the hard way.

DON PIPER
Pastor and author of *90 Minutes In Heaven*

*Anecdotes in this volume are based on fact;
however, in some instances, details have been
changed to protect some identities.*

Preface

1 John 1:9—*If we confess our sin, He is faithful and just and will forgive us our sin and cleanse us from all unrighteousness.*

Let me start off by first addressing what this book ISN'T. This book is NOT designed to condemn you for your past mistakes or to create some kind of guilt trip. Nor is this book intended to glorify sin or encourage anyone to sin all the more so that grace may abound.

But as you read through this book, please keep in mind that all mistakes, bad choices, or just plain thoughtless decisions you may have made in the past or are currently struggling with, can be overcome by the never-ending mercy and grace of Jesus Christ. Also, keep in mind that if you totally trust in Christ, His cleansing, forgiveness, and a fresh start are yours for the asking!

Now let me tell you what the book IS. My first and foremost objective is for you to develop a deeper and more meaningful relationship with Jesus Christ. My intent is to help you experience a paradigm shift—a change from one way of thinking to another—in relation to the age-old question that every student, young adult, and single person has asked on a very personal level: "How Far Is Too Far?"

Just show me in the Bible where it says word for word: DO NOT HAVE SEX BEFORE YOU'RE MARRIED!

I wanted an answer that made perfect sense, even when my walk with God wasn't perfect!

A Student Minister's Nightmare

Wow, where do I start? Let me tell you how this all came about. I was a rather wild child growing up, running free with very little discipline. I grew up in a single-parent home, and my mother worked her fingers to the bone to provide for my two brothers and me. She was a single mother raising three boys on a Louisiana teacher's salary—one of the lowest salaries in the country for teachers.

My two older brothers were absolutely great! They were eleven and seven years older than me, so you can see there were significant age differences between us. During most of my formative years it was just mom and me, because my two brothers had already moved out of the house.

If you were wondering what happened to my father, that story would take a whole book in itself. But I'll give you a little taste of that poison. The day I was to be born, my mom came home from work with severe labor pains, planning to have my father drive her to the hospital. She found him in bed with another woman. Needless to say, they got a divorce three months later on grounds of adultery.

When I was growing up, I tried to develop a relationship with my father, but he never showed much interest. Looking back, I realize that the Lord knew what He was doing by not allowing that relationship to grow. But it sure did hurt a lot at the time.

After discovering that it was, indeed, my father who had just been arrested for murder, I realized that God had rescued me from a world of disaster very early in life.

While I was in college, my economics professor called me into his office after class one day to discuss a private matter. Right then I was thinking, *Uh-oh—what did I do now?* But to my surprise, he threw down the front page of a newspaper and asked me if the man in the article was my father.

After discovering that it was, indeed, my father who had just been arrested for murder, I realized that God had rescued me from a world of disaster very early in life. At the age of fourteen, while I was visiting my father, he told me that I was as good as dead and to never contact him again. When I stood in my professor's office and remembered all the difficult times without an earthly father, it became crystal clear why the Lord had never allowed that relationship to flourish. I guess the God of all creation knows what He's doing. Enough said.

I have obviously left out a lot of details; not to mention, I jumped ahead a few years in the story. So let's rewind.

My mother, thank God, was a great Christian woman. One thing she did, regardless of how much I griped and complained, was make me go to church. Now I'm not talking about going to church once a week. I'm talking about going to church every time the doors were open! Some of you know what I mean—moms who make their kids go to church for Sunday school, youth choir, youth Bible study, visitation night, etc. Get the point? If the doors were open, I was there. If there was a church-sponsored sporting event, I was on the team. And just in case you still don't get it, on Wednesday nights when she was in adult choir practice, I was there, being baby-sat by the student minister, along with a few other kids who had moms like mine. Needless to say, by the age of fifteen I became a formidable expert on the rules and regulations pertaining to dodge ball!

Back then, I complained about going to church a lot. Looking back, I wouldn't change a thing. I thank God for my mom, and I thank her so much for having the discipline to build that foundation in my life. It really came in handy when the times got rough down the road.

When I was sixteen, and halfway through my junior year in high school, our church called a new student minister to serve. In my opinion, this man will now and forever be the greatest student minister in the history of student ministry. His name is Don Piper.

Don and I locked horns immediately. I will never forget our first confrontation. Don's wife, Eva, took the highly sought after job of starting and directing the youth choir. Did you detect a little sarcasm there? I thought so. Now, you need to understand that the majority of the youth at this church were generally interested in one thing—getting together and planning to do un-Christian activities as soon as church was over. Not to mention, for the guys, there were some pretty awesome-looking girls in the youth choir! Our agenda was definitely NOT to sing praise and worship hymns.

So, here I am on the back row, acting all cool and stuff—you know, acting as if I owned the place. Of course, I was trying to impress a beautiful little blonde in the soprano section. Her name was Connie.

This whole time, you could sense the frustration from Eva as she desperately tried to maintain control. You know the feeling you get when you think everything is going your way and nothing could possibly go wrong? I was having one of those moments—that is, until Don walked in, grabbed me by the back of the neck, and escorted me out in front of everyone. That's right—just when I was so close to getting Connie's phone number. Don proceeded to drag me down the hall, which was not a particularly easy thing to do. Not to brag or anything, but at the age of sixteen I could bench-press 225 pounds; and by age eighteen, I weighed in at a lean 185 pounds and was working out with 325 pounds on the bench. I guess you could say that, at times, Don had his work cut out for him. Not to mention, I was a complete and utter wise guy.

Anyhow, Don not only dragged me down the hall—he completely pulled me out of the building. Then he enlightened me on the biblical concept of how one's days on Earth could be shortened if one does not obey or respect those in authority. This was especially true when the particular authority figure just happens to be the student minister's wife! That night, Don and I reached an understanding of what my role would be in the youth group—period. But from that night forward, I knew I had been blessed with a father figure.

No one had ever spoken to me like that before. To this day, I still wonder how and where my life would have ended up if Don had never cared enough to take that initiative.

Several years later, Don shared with me that God had laid a strong burden on his heart from the first day he came to our church to visit. Even before Don actually joined the staff as our student minister, God had placed this burden on him concerning the fatherless young man that I was and my future ministry.

Don had even gone so far as to meet with my mother the first week he was employed, just to get the scoop on me and how best to minister to the needs in my life. I guess my mother must have shared a lot of information, because it was

> So at the early age of sixteen, I decided never again to think another impure, lustful, or physical thought about any female. I kept that resolution for about 7.01 seconds!

only a few days later that my first encounter with Don took place. Once again, God knew exactly what He was doing.

As my relationship with Don continued to develop, and he continued to grow as a minister, Don quickly learned what my number one weakness was. My biggest weakness also turned out to be THE major struggle in my life; it resulted in countless heartaches and hardships. I never struggled with the temptations of alcohol or drugs. Simply put, my biggest temptation was entirely directed toward members of the opposite sex—GIRLS!

Every major hardship or difficult situation I found myself in as a teenager or young adult was a direct result of bad decisions concerning girls. So at the early age of sixteen, I decided never again to think another impure, lustful, or physical thought about any female. I kept that resolution for about 7.01 seconds! Since that plan didn't work out so well, I went to Don for advice—and what followed is how all of this started.

You first need to understand that Don Piper was (and is) an extremely intelligent human being. He was highly educated and a very successful businessman before he completely lost his mind and gave up everything to follow God's calling into ministry. I say that as a little joke between Don and me. Don always told me: "Don't go into the ministry if there is ANYTHING else in life you can do that will make you happy." I realized that Don wasn't happy unless he was impacting lives in a profound way for Christ and glorifying God through the use of his gifts and talents. I guess that's why he gave up everything the world had to offer to follow Christ. I am so glad he did!

There's another thing you should know about Don. He has a very competitive streak in him that I like to refer to as the *Debate Syndrome.* Don was a member of award-winning debate teams in high school and college. He took great pride in learning as much as possible about a particular subject before he ever discussed it or presented it as a sermon at church. If you challenged his expertise, you were in for a very lengthy debate. Such debates would often continue into lunch or dinner at his favorite Italian restaurant over fettuccini with cream sauce, garlic bread, and iced tea. You can probably see where this is going. I challenged Don a lot—anything for a free meal!

Although I never suffered from *Debate Syndrome,* I was definitely a member of the Forget-To-Think-Before-You-Speak Club. More often than not, I would say what I thought and then wish I'd never said it in the first place. But once it came out of my mouth, I would defend my point no matter how wrong it was! I would keep on pressing the issue until the other party just gave up. But Don would never give up!

I'll never forget when I was a junior in high school and went to Don with the question that every student minister faces at one point or another. The answers he gave me were NOT what I wanted to hear. So I quickly challenged those answers, and the debate was on!

> **Please tell me—is there anywhere in the Bible where it tells you exactly HOW FAR IS TOO FAR?**

Here's how it all went down—I walked into Don's office after school one day. He could tell that I looked a little stressed and downhearted. He asked, "What's wrong?" I said, "Don, you know I have been dating Lauren for a while, and I'm really struggling with the pressures to do some things that I feel might not be right. First of all, I really think that I love her. Second, we have already done some things that I am sort of wondering if we should have done in the first place. But to be honest, it was totally awesome! And I think I want to do even more! Just put yourself in my place. Don, you've seen Lauren! She's like one of the hottest girls in school, and she wants me to go all the way! What do I do? Please tell me—is there **anywhere** in the Bible where it tells you **exactly** *HOW FAR IS TOO FAR?*"

So, there it was. Hanging in the air was the question that every student minister loves, longs for, and prays earnestly to hear on a daily basis. (Yeah, right! They would probably rather have root canals without the nitrous than answer that question!) It was staring him right in the face. Don looked stumped. For once, he had nothing to say. I had won! The impossible had happened, or so I thought. Then Don spoke.

At first, he started with the standard stuff to break the ice. You know, student minister things like, "Hey, I know exactly what you mean. I feel your pain, man. I think I know what you're going through. I read about this exact situation in a class in seminary. I think it was called 'The Difficult Questions Students Ask And The Answers You Need To Give Because You Won't Have A Clue How To Relate To Them.'" (Just kidding around again!)

Seriously though, Don started to explain how important and sacred sexual purity is to the bond of marriage. He then continued to share how we all go through struggles and temptations of varying degrees and that, if we trust in Jesus, everything will make perfect sense. Looking back on that moment, Don did a better job of handling that situation than most people would have done.

At one point he opened up his Bible and started to read the following verses:

> **1 Corinthians 10:13**—*No temptation has seized you except what is common to man. And God is faithful; he will not let you be tempted beyond what you can bear. But when you are tempted, he will also provide a way out so that you can stand up under it.*

9

1 Corinthians 6:18-20—*Flee from sexual immorality. All other sins a man commits are outside his body, but he who sins sexually sins against his own body. [19]Do you not know that your body is a temple of the Holy Spirit, who is in you, whom you have received from God? You are not your own; [20]you were bought at a price. Therefore honor God with your body.*

Ephesians 5:3—*But among you there must not be even a hint of sexual immorality, or of any kind of impurity, or of greed, because these are improper for God's holy people.*

1 Corinthians 6:13b—*The body is not meant for sexual immorality, but for the Lord, and the Lord for the body.*

1 Thessalonians 4:3-5—*It is God's will that you should be sanctified: that you should avoid sexual immorality; [4]that each of you should learn to control his own body in a way that is holy and honorable, [5]not in passionate lust like the heathen, who do not know God;*

Matthew 5:28—*But I tell you that anyone who looks at a woman lustfully has already committed adultery with her in his heart.*

As Don read each verse, he explained them in detail and brought them to life. He continued to pour out his feelings and passion for sexual purity. Don let me know that he genuinely wanted to help me through this matter.

But that's not what I wanted to hear! I wanted to hear that if you really think you're "in love," then it's OK to have those thoughts and to act on those desires. So, as he read each verse, I debated heatedly. Getting frustrated, I had a rebuttal for every line. My comments and thoughts were like these:

- Come on, Don. I'm not being immoral.
- I really love this girl. She means everything to me.
- It's not like I want to commit some kind of sexual crime.
- I'm not doing anything unnatural.
- I just want her to know how much I really love her.
- I honestly think this is the girl I might marry one day.
- I'm not lusting after her. I really care about her.
- I'm not committing adultery. Neither one of us is married.
- PLEASE, I want a verse that literally hits me over the head with a two-by-four.
- Why can't there be a chapter in the Bible that specifically tells you what you can and can't do when you're dating?
- Just show me in the Bible where it says word for word: DO NOT HAVE SEX BEFORE YOU'RE MARRIED!

Again, I thought I had him stumped. This time he didn't debate me. He just sat there quietly and let me ramble on.

When I was finally finished, an uneasy silence filled the room. He then asked a question that hit me right between the eyes: "Todd, where are you in your spiritual walk?"

Knowing the answer but stalling for time, I asked him what he meant. He asked me, "Are you spending at least five minutes a day reading Scripture and praying to God?" Of course at this point, I had to say no. Then he said, "I'll tell you what. Why don't you commit to five minutes a day reading Scripture and praying to God for one week—and when that week is over, we'll continue this discussion."

> I'll define the "gray areas" as the times in our lives when we allow that intimate relationship with God to be reduced to a casual acquaintance.

Even though I agreed to take Don up on his five-minute challenge, I thought his response was an utter cop-out. I still wanted something more . . . **I wanted an answer that made perfect sense, even when my walk with God wasn't perfect!**

Needless to say, after that week passed, I really didn't feel like discussing the issue any longer. After spending more time focusing on God than on Lauren, I found that I really didn't have much of an argument.

Isn't it amazing that when we allow ourselves to slip away from that intimate and personal relationship with God, things become sort of gray and hazy? I'll define the "gray areas" as the times in our lives when we allow that intimate relationship with God to be reduced to a casual acquaintance. These are the times when it's difficult to determine absolute truth. The obvious becomes vague. It's hard to determine wrong from right—it's complicated to see in terms of black and white. It is during these times we find it easy to straddle the fence and just go with the flow, taking a stand for nothing. It is during the gray areas of our lives that we are at our most vulnerable point. This is the time Satan loves the most—he finds it easy to trick us into falling for his lies and temptations.

Because I constantly dwelled in the gray areas, it was easy to take the Scriptures Don read and argue every line. Those Scriptures are so powerful that alone they could stomp out any argument or debate concerning premarital sex or physical intimacy! But I still had the audacity to believe I was smart enough to take the Word of God (the Creator of the Universe) and distort His infallible Truth into whatever I wanted it to mean for my particular situation and satisfaction. Sound familiar?

At times, I find it hard to believe I'm a creation of a perfect God when I look at all the stupid mistakes I've made. I wonder if God just looks down at me, laughs, and thinks, *Could I have made ONE mistake?* OK—we all know God is perfect! Good thing He is in the business of forgiving.

Basically, I was doing what a lot of you are doing with your lives right now. I was placing more emphasis on everything around me than on my relationship with God.

The Roller-Coaster Ride Begins

I wish I could tell you that everything turned out great from that day forward. But that wouldn't be true. So, allow me to continue.

Starting my senior year in high school, the temptations just kept on coming. Let me paint you a picture of my senior year. You might want to sit down for what I am about to tell you, because it may be a little too much for some of you to handle. Here it is: I was a male cheerleader. But I can guarantee I wasn't doing it to promote school spirit.

I don't know if it's still the same in high school now, but when I was there, the girls who were voted onto the cheerleading squad were typically the most popular and best looking in school. I know there's a biblical verse that talks about fleeing from your youthful lust and desires, but I thought I could handle anything. Instead of fleeing, I chose to camp out, right smack in the middle of mine! Oh yeah, here's that verse—you might want to check it out!

2 Timothy 2:22—*Flee the evil desires of youth, and pursue righteousness, faith, love, and peace, along with those who call on the Lord out of a pure heart.*

Let me explain in a little more detail how my cheerleading career came about. First, I was ineligible to play any sports my junior year in high school. I had made some bad decisions during the first six weeks of my freshman year. I was running with a rough crowd and I got into a lot of trouble. My grades went right down the toilet.

My mother promptly had me transferred to another school where she just happened to be a teacher—that way she could monitor my every move. Try to imagine that—Here I am a teenager, trying to fit in with the "in-crowd," and I have to ride to and from school every day with my mother! And to top it off, I couldn't play sports. I was not a happy camper. The district in which I was attending school would not allow sports eligibility for a full calendar year following a transfer from another school within the same district. That policy prevented schools from recruiting athletes from one another.

So there I was—a freshman where my mother was teaching—and I couldn't do the one thing that I loved, which was play football! Instead of football, I decided to study and prove to Mom that I was a safe risk. It worked! After two long years of being in my mother's shadow, after two long years of studying so hard I thought my brain was going to explode, after two long years of working to raise my GPA from a 1.0 during my first six weeks as a freshman to a 3.75—I was free! My mother granted permission for me to return to my old stomping grounds for my junior year. And the roller-coaster ride began.

Even though I was heading back to school with all my old friends, things were not the same. You know how that out-of-sight, out-of-mind thing works, right? For two years I had been away, doing my best to make other friends. So even though I was back home, I was the new kid in town again. It was like starting all over.

The friends that I was hanging around with during my freshman year didn't hold the same attraction for me. I actually found myself wanting a good future. I wanted to surround myself with the best people I could find. For some reason I actually wanted to keep my nose clean. Go figure!

It's sort of like this: Imagine removing a gang member from his gang and throwing him into the military for two years. After two years of strict discipline and mental training, you cast him back into his old gang with the same old members—he ain't gonna fit! That's exactly how I felt. I no longer clicked with my old running buddies.

Fortunately, one of the members in our church had two children, Kayla and Kyle, who attended the high school that I was returning to. I had known Kyle from playing YMCA football together throughout elementary school. Kayla didn't play football—duh. But she and all her friends were part of the cheerleading squad for our team. They were our cheerleaders from first grade through sixth grade. Kayla was one year older and one grade ahead of her brother Kyle and me.

Now, Kyle was a great guy. He was very talented and incredibly smart, but we didn't have that much in common except for his sister.

On the flip side, Kayla was one of the best-looking girls in school. This girl defined hot. Not only was she the most popular girl in school, but she was also the captain of the cheerleading squad. So naturally, all her friends were other cheerleaders. Her best friend during high school was named Nicole. Nicole was not only a gorgeous red-head, she was also highly intelligent and co-captain of the cheerleading squad. She had the total package. I didn't mean to squeeze Kyle out or anything, but it didn't take a rocket scientist to see where my focus on this brother-sister friendship was being directed.

Things were starting out great my junior year. My high school had just hired a new head football coach. Our new coach had started his education career several years earlier as a teacher with my mother. When I was just a wee lad, he would occasionally help my mom out by babysitting me—granting my mom a little peace and quiet. So, the coach and I knew each other quite well.

This was great! Even though I was ineligible to play football my junior year, I was able to participate in the weight-training program with the team. My closest friends were the most popular girls in school, I got to work out with the football team, and the head coach loved me. Life was good!

Since I was unable to play any school sports, I decided to take gymnastic classes at the local gym. Of course, there was also a hidden agenda in that decision. Kayla shared that a lot of cheerleading squads attended that gym to train for regional competitions. So, my buddy Mark and I started taking lessons once a week. We actually became rather skilled at floor tumbling. Since we had strategically positioned ourselves to be the only guys in the tumbling classes, we were asked by the instructors to help spot for the other cheerleaders. In addition, the members of the cheerleading squads wanted us to help them train and learn stunts in order to prepare them for college. Needless to say, Mark and I were more than happy to help these young ladies in their time of need, and this always led to some interesting relationships.

At that time, the state of Louisiana did not have a public school with male cheerleaders. So Kayla and Nicole devised a plan and petitioned the school

> Just imagine being one of only six guys trapped on a college campus for an entire week with over 1,200 cheerleaders.

board for our high school to be the first public school to have male cheerleaders. The school board approved their request, and Kayla and Nicole made history. Little did

I know that Mark and I were going to be a part of that history! The tryouts were held, and we became cheerleaders. It was a tough job (working with all those beautiful girls)—but like they say—someone has to do it!

Shortly after finishing my junior year, I was leaving for UCA Cheerleading Camp! Just imagine being one of only six guys trapped on a college campus for an entire week with over twelve hundred cheerleaders. It was awesome!

Since we were the only guys at the cheerleading camp, they hadn't planned where we would stay during the week. So the camp coordinators gave us the top floor in one of the dorms where six hundred girls were staying! That was not a good idea . . . Anyhow, the week proved to be extremely challenging on a physical level (cheerleading is not easy; it is hard work and at times can be dangerous), not to mention the psychological torture that went along with being surrounded by twelve hundred girls for six days. But somehow I still managed to develop several relationships that later wrecked my priorities for the rest of my senior year.

My senior year continued as a spiritual roller-coaster ride. There were many ups and downs, twists and turns, and the occasional loop-the-loop that left my stomach or my heart splattered on a wall somewhere. Don was still playing an active role in my life as a student minister and father figure. We stayed close during that year, but it was on a different level. I was still attending church; it's just that I didn't allow myself to get too close to Don. He was a constant reminder of where my spiritual walk should be, and I was nowhere close to walking with God.

Looking back now, it's crystal clear why I hardened my heart not only to Don, but also to my mother, my family, and most of my friends. I knew God was calling me to serve Him and that I should be using this time to prepare my life for the ministry. But I allowed myself to be tempted and seduced by all the things of this world. In essence, I was playing with fire, and we all know what happens when you play with fire. Sooner or later you WILL get burned. I still have the scars . . .

I continued to struggle with temptations throughout high school. I made more mistakes than I care to mention. My spiritual walk was constantly up and down. I would straighten up for a while and see the light, and then another temptation would catch my wandering eye. This became a regular pattern in my life. Many of those who were close to me could see it so clearly, yet I was completely blind to it.

Basically, I was doing what a lot of you are doing with your lives right now. I was placing more emphasis on everything around me than on my relationship with God. I didn't have time to spend five minutes a day praying and reading God's Word. And if the truth were told, I wasn't sure that I wanted to make the time. After that whirlwind of a senior year, it was time for college.

God is merciful. His grace transcends all things. As children of the King, healing and forgiveness are always available. God can and often does use ALL things to work for the good of those who love Him. But our choices DO matter. His forgiveness does NOT erase the consequences of our sinful choices, nor does it prevent the scars.

Let me tell you from personal experience: trying to fight the battle against sexual temptation without the armor of God is a losing proposition from the start.

The College Years

I f you're a high school student reading this, hear me well. It does NOT get easier in college. As a matter of fact, the temptations and struggles that you will face could very well wreck your life if you are not anchored in the solid rock of Jesus Christ. College made the struggles I faced in high school seem like child's play. When I started college, another level of temptation was thrown into my face—the deceptively tantalizing world of fraternity/sorority parties, dance clubs, and bars. This was a whole new way to meet and develop dysfunctional relationships with girls.

I won't bore you with all the details, but to say the least, I dove right into the deep end. When I was in college, you only had to be eighteen to legally drink alcohol. Now, take all those same temptations that I had been unsuccessfully struggling with over the past couple of years and throw alcohol into the mix. Man—I had some messed-up situations staring me right in the face. I think you get the picture. Needless to say, I spent a lot of time walking the aisle at church, kneeling at the altar, and asking God to forgive me for some very stupid decisions.

God is merciful. His grace transcends all things. As children of the King, healing and forgiveness are always available. God can and often does use ALL things to work for the good of those who love Him. But our choices DO matter. His forgiveness does NOT erase the **consequences** of our sinful choices, nor does it prevent the **scars.** Please remember these truths!

I want to share a pivotal point in my life that took place during this downturn. After completing my freshman year in college, I left for basic training and AIT (Advanced Individual Training) in the army. That's right—I made a very grown-up decision to instill some discipline in my life. Actually, it was to pay for my college. I joined the Louisiana Army National Guard and was shipped off for training. That was one of the best things I could have done! I was away from members of the opposite sex for seventeen weeks. That was clearly the most difficult part of the training!

> We started dating, and that eventually turned into an exclusive arrangement. You know, the kind where you have "The Talk."

When I returned, I immediately met a girl. Does that surprise you? Her name was Kelly. Actually, I had met Kelly several years earlier while attending a church youth camp. Since common ground had been established years earlier, she quickly agreed to go on a date.

Kelly and I hit it off great! We started dating, and that eventually turned into an exclusive arrangement. You know, the kind where you have "The Talk." The Talk can be defined as when two people involved in a relationship cut open their chests, rip out their hearts, and share secrets about their pasts that no one else needs to know. Then, based on the outcome, each party decides if he or she still likes one another. **By the way, this is not a good thing for two insecure people to do.**

Kelly and I dated for about a year, which was the longest dating relationship I had established up to that point in my life. Although Kelly and I were convinced that we were totally in love, our relationship did anything BUT glorify God. Don't get me wrong; she was a great girl. It's just that Satan has a way of taking two good people and bringing out the very worst in them. We were so caught up in each other's wants and desires that we left God completely out of our relationship—which made it easy to succumb to that age-old temptation every young man and woman faces—and that got us in more trouble than you can imagine! Let me tell you from personal experience: trying to fight the battle against sexual temptation without the armor of God is a losing proposition from the start.

Ephesians 6:10–18—*Finally, be strong in the Lord and in his mighty power. [11]Put on the full armor of God so that you can take your stand against the devil's schemes. [12]For our struggle is not against flesh and blood, but against* *the rulers, against the authorities, against the powers of this dark world and against the spiritual forces of evil in the heavenly realms. [13]Therefore put on the full armor of God, so that when the day of evil comes, you may be able to stand your ground, and after you have done everything, to stand. [14]Stand firm then, with the belt of truth buckled around your waist, with the breastplate of righteousness in place, [15]and with your feet fitted with the readiness that comes from the gospel of peace. [16]In addition to all this, take up the shield of faith, with which you can extinguish all the flaming arrows of the evil one. [17]Take the helmet of salvation and the sword of the Spirit, which is the word of God. [18]And pray in the Spirit on all occasions with all kinds of prayers and requests. With this in mind, be alert and always keep on praying for all the saints.*

While my relationship with Kelly was slowly destroying my life (as a result of participating in un-Christian activities), I had another saga developing. One of my mother's favorite students, whom she taught through high school, was going through a rather difficult time at home. His parents were fighting and heading for a messy divorce. Michael's parents asked my mother if he could stay with us for a few months while they tried to salvage their marriage.

I thought it would be great! It was like having a younger brother. Michael was two years younger than me, and Kelly fell right in the middle of us in terms of age. Like me, Michael was athletic and outgoing. He also suffered from insecurity and dealt with his self-esteem issues through the girls he dated or chose to be seen with.

So Michael moved in with us, and our relationship became very strong. I loved him like a brother. I actually think I was closer to him than to my own

> You guessed it. The car he borrowed from me, and the money I gave him, were being used to date Kelly.

brothers at the time. I would give Michael money so he could go out and party; and at times, I would even let him borrow my car on the nights I had to work late.

Little did I know, after living in my house for over three months and having Kelly around all the time, they were developing a very close friendship. Yep, you guessed it. The car he borrowed from me, and the money I gave him, were being used to date Kelly. I found out in a very difficult way; and to make a long story short, I not only lost the girl I thought I was in love with, but I also lost the closest friend I ever had.

I can't begin to tell you how painful that experience was. Just writing about it brings back some very deep-rooted feelings. It was a horrible situation, but GOD spared me from doing anything drastic.

After that experience, I went almost an entire year in college without dating a girl! I know it's hard to believe, because up until that point my life obviously revolved around girls. Instead, I immersed myself in God's Word, getting very active in the Baptist Student Union on campus and as a college worker with the student ministry at my church.

By this time, Don Piper had moved on from our church to a church in Houston, Texas, where he was now the associate pastor. We stayed in close contact, and on a regular basis I would drive down to visit him and his family. I struggled deeply with the idea that God had placed a calling on my life for ministry. Over the next year, I took counsel with leaders in my church, my pastor, and Don on a regular basis. Toward the end of college, I decided to surrender to God's call to ministry.

But Satan had other plans. I had always enjoyed singing and performing. While in college, I performed at several community events, local beauty pageants, and churches. As I was struggling with my call to ministry, I was asked to perform for a major event on our college campus. I mean, all the TV and radio stations were there! Our campus was opened to the entire public; this was a BIG deal! Even the governor of Louisiana and newly seated members of the legislature were attending! On top of that, over thirty high schools were present for cheerleading and dance line competitions. Can you picture that scene? The campus was bursting at the seams with people. Cheerleading squads, dance line teams, students, parents, family members, politicians, and the general public had invaded our college campus!

In the fall of 1991, country music was EXPLODING! But I wanted no part of it. I was big-time into rock-n-roll. I listened to all the rock bands: Aerosmith, Bon Jovi, Boston, Def Leppard, Foreigner, Journey, Kansas, Motley Crue, Poison, Styx, U2, Van Halen, and a few heavy metal Christian bands. I tried to stay well rounded in the rock department. The only country musicians I even knew existed at the time were Randy Travis, Ricky Van Shelton, Travis Tritt, and Garth Brooks—I knew these only because my mom was such a huge fan.

Despite my lack of love for country music, the coordinators for this event insisted that I learn TWENTY country songs. I got this news rather suddenly on the Wednesday night before the event (two days before), when they discovered that their first choice for the entertainment had developed strep throat and would be unable to perform. Needless to say, I got acquainted with country music fast!

At that point in my life, it was by far the largest audience for which I had ever performed. I got noticed. The general manager of a local radio station, who was attending the event, asked if I had any original songs available for on-air play. Before I knew it, I had songs on the radio, and I was a featured opening act for area promotional events. That radio station even sponsored my very own concert at the civic center in my hometown. The concert sold out! Things were happening fast.

As a result of this newfound popularity, I was distracted once again. I lost my focus on God. Looking back now, I see how Satan used this to continue the destructive patterns in my life. It still amazes me how you can give a normal guy a microphone and put him on a stage, and then watch girls lose all sense of reason. To this day I still don't understand that.

In any case, the cycle continued. I was right back on the destructive course I had started several years earlier. My eyes were off the Lord and His purposes for my life. I had once again traded things of eternal value and importance for the temporary pleasures of earthly things. And now I had found other tools to attract the opposite sex: a guitar, a microphone, and a cowboy hat.

A producer from Nashville, Tennessee, took a strong interest in me. So, during my last semester in college, I was traveling back and forth to Nashville, recording and developing as an artist. Shortly after I graduated from college, I moved to Music City.

Mark my words: if you allow yourself to date a nonbeliever in the hope that you will lead them to Christ, inevitably your walk with God will be crippled.

I saw myself as someone worthy to serve God—not because of anything I had accomplished, but rather, because of what Jesus had accomplished for me!

Face Down on the Floor

So there I was in Nashville—Music City, USA. I had left Louisiana as a big fish in a small pond, and then quickly discovered I was a tiny minnow in a big sea. So many musicians and artists there had more talent in one little finger than I had in my entire body! But somehow, doors continued to open. Two weeks before I arrived in Nashville, I had actually negotiated a production/publishing deal with a music company. In no time at all, I was working with some very established songwriters, singing in local clubs, and recording in studios. It seemed as if everything were going just as I had planned.

But once again, disaster was lurking around the corner . . . in a tight skirt. That's right. I was stupid enough to start a relationship with a girl who worked for the same production company. Jennifer was actually a great girl, but in me she had found what possibly was the right guy at the wrong time.

At that particular time in my life, I was a little too big for my britches, so I thought I could get away with anything. Jennifer demanded that I straighten up and refocus my efforts on developing a personal relationship with Jesus. She was yet another voice telling me that I was running from God and that I needed to get my life back on track. But I was more concerned with seeking stardom than surrendering all to Jesus at the time.

Unfortunately, my actions caught up with me, and my relationship with Jennifer ended rather ugly! Since Jennifer worked for the production company, and I was easily replaceable by one of thousands of talented singer/songwriters, the executive producer thought it was best that we end our arrangement and go our separate ways.

I see now that this was actually a good thing, because it started the process whereby I began preparing my heart once again to seek God's will for my life. After discovering that I was unable to get other music companies to make the same kind of arrangement I had when I first moved to Nashville, I was extremely humbled.

As a result of my newfound humility, I started working various odd jobs around town to pay bills. I actually got lucky on a few of them. On one occasion, I was asked to audition for a television commercial for a clothing store, and I got the job! As a result, I appeared in more than five television commercials the following year. In turn, that led to one other job offer: I was hired as a "Fit Model" for a major clothing manufacturer. I couldn't believe it! I was actually the size 32 Fit Model for a clothing line for two years! How cool was that? OK, I know I keep reflecting back on the days when I was in good shape. I really need to get back in the gym and start working out!

Let's move on to a significant turning point that happened in my life as a result of those odd jobs. One of the jobs I tried was working for an automotive dealer. That's right—I was selling cars.

Until that point, I had been in Nashville for about a year and a half and had never bothered to attend church, except during the occasional visit back home. One day a guy walked into the dealership and wanted to buy a new vehicle. I waited on him. During the time we spent searching for the perfect car, we learned a lot about each other. He was a Christian with a heart for Jesus, and he was not afraid to share how he felt with others.

While we were test-driving his new car, the customer asked me if I were a Christian. I told him yes, although I had not been living like one. Then he asked if I attended a local church; I replied that I had not yet found a church home. In reality, I had not been looking! You see, I was completely on my own in Nashville. The only friends or acquaintances I had developed were through my relationship with Jennifer and her family. Since that relationship had been severed, I was really a bit of a loner. Anyway, the customer invited me to his church for a Christmas pageant. I accepted his offer. God showed up, blessed and convicted my heart, and I began attending that church. It was there that I was introduced to a man named Doug Haley.

> But somehow, once again, Satan intervened . . . He introduced a pretty blue-eyed blonde.

Doug was teaching the ninth- and tenth-grade boys' Sunday school class. Shortly after meeting Doug, I expressed to him my desire to help with the youth department. I explained to him that I had been actively involved in my youth group at church while growing up, and that I knew the Lord had placed a strong burden on my heart to work with teenagers. Doug and I met a few more times, and he unselfishly asked if I would like to help in teaching his Sunday school class.

We had an amazing group of young men in that Sunday school class, and God enabled me to develop strong relationships with many of them. God had blessed me with the ability to reach them on their level, continuing the affirmation that He had truly called me to serve in the area of student ministry.

But somehow, once again, Satan intervened . . . He introduced a pretty, blue-eyed blonde—ironically, her name was also Jennifer. And she was NOT a good influence in my life.

Have you ever found yourself in a relationship solely because you thought you could help someone grow closer to God by dating him or her? You know, we call it missionary dating. If you have been lucky enough so far to be spared from this horrible dilemma, DON'T GO THERE!

The Bible clearly describes this in 2 Corinthians 6:14–18. These verses, if followed whole-heartedly, can save you from a great deal of pain and heartache in your life. Please read them carefully!

2 Corinthians 6:14–18—*Do not be yoked together with unbelievers. For what do righteousness and wickedness have in common? Or what fellowship can light have with darkness? 15What harmony is there between Christ and Belial? What does a believer have in common with an unbeliever? 16What agreement is there between the temple of God and idols? For we are the temple of the living God. As God has said: "I will live with them and walk among them, and I will be their God, and they will be my people." 17"Therefore come out from them and be separate, says the Lord. Touch no unclean thing, and I will receive you." 18"I will be a Father to you, and you will be my sons and daughters, says the Lord Almighty."*

These are the verses that specifically advise us NOT to get deeply involved with nonbelievers. Mark my words: if you allow yourself to date nonbelievers in the hope that you will lead them to Christ, inevitably your walk with God will be crippled. It is far easier for them to pull you down than for you to pull them up. All right, back to the story.

Jennifer #2 and I continued on yet another path of mutual destruction. Luckily, while I was working at another job after leaving the car dealership, an angel walked into my life. To this day, I believe she was an angel sent from Heaven to FINALLY help someone too stupid to help himself. This angel's name was Stephanie.

Stephanie and I immediately developed a kind of relationship that I had never before experienced with a female. Although she was an incredibly beautiful young woman with an amazing singing voice, I found myself looking at a girl, for the very first time in my life, as a beautiful creation of God instead of some kind of trophy. This was a whole new ball game!

As our relationship continued to grow, I would dive deeper into my past and share more of my history. I was beginning to understand what it meant to be a brother and sister in Christ. Stephanie was truly a Spiritual Sister in Christ.

One night, after grabbing a bite to eat, Stephanie invited me to her apartment. She said she had something God had placed on her heart to share with me. She started by recognizing the fact that I was caught in a destructive cycle. She then boldly confronted me on that issue and demanded to know WHY I had continued down the same road over and over again!

I opened up and finally shared with her how I really felt about myself as a person. I stated the following with a huge lump in my throat: "I have messed up so many times that I have come to the conclusion it is just not worth trying anymore. I mean, what girl in her right mind would want anything to do with a guy like me? I want to marry a Christian girl one day, but what right do I have to even ask God for such a special privilege? Let's get real: a good Christian girl has obviously been praying that God would bring her a great Christian guy. So, what on earth could she ever see in me?"

> Have you forgotten that almost every great man of God in the Bible FAILED God miserably at first? They only became great AFTER they surrendered ALL to God!

The response she gave me would forever change my life!

Stephanie said, "You're right, Todd. Good Christian girls do pray that God will bring them just that—a good Christian guy! But, Todd, have you read your Bible lately? Have you forgotten that almost every great man of God in the Bible **FAILED** God miserably at first? They only became great **AFTER** they surrendered **ALL** to God! Just look at David. He committed murder and adultery before he became a man after God's own heart. Look at Paul. He actually murdered Christians before he became the man that God used to write most of the New Testament and reach most of the then-known world for Christ! Todd, God can still use you in a profound way if you will just give **everything to HIM!** Like many girls, I have been praying since I was little that God would bring me a great Christian guy. I mean, just look at me—I'm twenty-four years old and still a virgin. Believe me—the temptations and struggles have been just as hard for me as for anyone. But if I were to place stipulations and guidelines on the man God has planned for me, based on my human wants and desires, I could miss out on a David or a Paul. **Who am I as a servant of God to question God's choice for me?"**

Right then my life was changed. What she said totally blew me away! I looked at myself in a whole new light. I looked at myself in the newness of God, clothed not in the filth of my own past, but in the righteousness of Christ! I looked at myself as a new creation of God. I saw myself as someone worthy to serve God—not because of anything I had accomplished, but rather, because of what Jesus had accomplished for me! Because of the blood of Christ, I could be that man of God that some woman somewhere would be proud to accept as the man she had been praying for. I will never forget the impact Stephanie made on my life and the words of wisdom God gave her that night. Those words changed me profoundly.

After I left Stephanie's apartment that night, I ended that destructive relationship with Jennifer #2. When I called Stephanie and shared the news, she resounded with a hardy, Praise God! I then told her I was leaving the next morning to travel home for a week or so to collect my thoughts and spend some time with my family and friends. She made me promise that I would stop by her apartment on my way out of town. I asked why, and she said, "It's a surprise!"

The next morning I got up and got ready for my trip back home. When I stopped by Stephanie's apartment, she met me at the door and handed me two cassette tapes. I asked her what they were, and she said, "That's your surprise! Just promise me you will listen to them. I know you have a special love for music, so I made a couple of tapes with some songs I thought would help you deal with what you're going through." I gave her a big hug and I promised her I would listen.

With the skyline of Nashville in my rear-view mirror, I traveled down I-40 toward Memphis. I popped in the first cassette.

> When I walked through the door, I literally fell face down on the floor.

The songs were beautiful, extremely inspirational, and my heart was completely open to their meaning.

It seemed as if God had created that day just for me. The scenery was absolutely breathtaking! I had seen it a hundred times before, but this time it was God's hand I saw in everything. As the songs played, I traveled on, and about seventy miles west of Nashville I put in the second tape. A new and beautiful melody began to play.

The piano licks were incredible, and it seemed as though the singer was singing to me alone. His amazing voice caught my attention. But it was the lyrics that captivated my soul. When the singer reached the chorus and sang the words, *I Surrender All,* my heart literally broke. I pulled over to the side of the interstate and wept.

I played the song over and over again while my heart continued to break for God. After listening to the song for what seemed like a solid hour, I drove to the next exit, turned around, and headed back to my apartment in Nashville. When I walked through the door, I literally fell face down on the floor. I wept uncontrollably and begged God for another chance to serve His kingdom and glorify His Name.

I lay there for almost seven hours, crying until there were no more tears to cry. It was then that I knew what Don Piper meant years ago when he told me, "If you keep running from God, He WILL get your attention! And when He does, you'll find yourself face down on the floor before HIM!" That's when it finally hit me and I truly understood the following statement: God will help those who are too stupid to help themselves.

Exhausted and dehydrated, it took everything I had to pick myself up off the floor. I walked over to the phone and called Don, who was now a pastor in Plano, Texas. When he heard the brokenness in my voice, he immediately asked,

"You've finally reached that point, haven't you?"

I said, "Yes."

Don asked what I was doing for the next couple of days, and I told him I was coming to see him! He said, "Come on." I drove to Texas and stayed about a week. He counseled with me, we prayed together, and we both came to the conclusion that God was definitely calling me to the ministry. The time to surrender had come. I had finally stopped running.

I need something that answers the question, 'How Far Is Too Far?' without leaving any room for doubt.

What Goes around Comes Around

after returning to Nashville, I sought counsel with the pastor at the church where Doug and I taught Sunday school. The pastor knew my abilities and agreed that God had called me to serve in the area of student ministry. So the following Sunday, I walked the aisle and stood before the congregation to make my decision known publicly before my church family. The wheels were set in motion, and God started opening doors for ministry opportunities very quickly!

Shortly after I surrendered to God's calling on my life, our church decided to hire a new student minister. They called a godly man who came highly recommended—his name was Robbie Robison.

Robbie was one of the most dynamic and energetic human beings I had ever met. He had an incredible ability to touch the hearts of every student with whom he made contact. And he did just that—he made it a priority to impact every student in that youth group, which was no small feat. When Robbie started, the average attendance of the group was around 70 to 80 students per week—within three months, the student ministry grew to over 170 students! God showed up in a big way and used Robbie to impact students' lives.

Robbie and I developed a very close friendship immediately. He took me under his wing, so to speak, and began to coach and teach me about the inner workings of developing a successful student ministry. God continued to use Doug and me to teach. Our relationships with the students continued to grow, and lives were being impacted for Christ. These young men were coming to know Jesus as their Savior and Lord. It was incredible!

One day, out of nowhere, Robbie asked if I had ever felt God's calling to full-time student ministry. When I said yes, he proceeded to tell me of a local church that was looking for a student minister. Robbie knew the pastor and thought he would be great to work under for my first position as a church staff member.

At first I was very nervous. I didn't think I was ready, but Robbie had a few words of wisdom. He said, "Just relax, Todd. God has been preparing you for ministry all of your life—you just didn't know it. Dude, you have an amazing ability with students, and your heart is on fire to reach young people for Christ. Trust in God and the gifts He has given you, and your ministry will be blessed beyond your wildest imagination."

Can you guess whom I called for advice? You're right—
Don Piper. After extensive prayer and counseling, Don
and I knew that God had opened this door for me and that
I had to walk through it. So Robbie arranged a meeting
with the pastor he had told me about, Mike Adams. I knew
from our very first meeting that Mike was a true man of
God. After a few minutes of conversation, we both knew
that God had brought us together.

Mike and I visited on several different occasions, and
he decided that it was time

> I felt like Neo dodging
> bullets in *The Matrix!*

to move forward with my application for the position of
student minister. I was asked to meet the search committee
(a group of men, usually deacons and elders in the church,
whose sole responsibility is to make a candidate feel as
nervous as possible).

I will never forget meeting that committee for the first
time. I walked into a room full of elderly men sitting in
a big semicircle, and I was asked to take a chair right in
the middle of them. What had I gotten myself into? They
started firing questions at me in rapid succession. I felt
like Neo dodging bullets in *The Matrix!*

Just imagine that scenario for a moment. I was being
asked about everything from my past experiences to my
vision for the future. I think I lost about ten pounds by
the time that meeting was over! But God had His hand

on the meeting, and it went great! I held nothing back. These godly men viewed me for who I was and where my heart was right then. The chairman of the search committee actually stood up and said, "You're exactly what our young people need. I don't approve of your past, but I believe that you know what the young people in today's world struggle with, and I believe that you can reach them and relate to them on a whole new level."

My heart was so touched. And then an amazing thing happened. The men stood up, walked over to me, and we all joined in prayer asking God to anoint the decision that had to be made concerning the student ministry at that church. You could feel the presence of the Holy Spirit in the room! A few days later, after meeting with the board of deacons, the church extended what was known as the in view of a call invitation. Can you believe that only seven months after surrendering to God's calling in my life, I was "auditioning" for a church? I was actually going to speak and get voted on by a church—God sure doesn't waste any time! After I spoke, the church met and voted. Later that day, Mike called me with the news. I had been elected as their new student minister. God is awesome!

After starting my new job as a full-time student minister, God really started to work fast. The church in which I was serving was located directly across the street from one of the largest high schools in the state of Tennessee. This school was huge—It actually had four schools on one campus: North, South, East, and West. Each school had over eight hundred students!

I immediately began strategizing a plan to get involved on campus at this high school. I knew there would be tons of ministry opportunities. Luckily, God had already laid a foundation for me at the school. Several years earlier, while I was singing and performing, I was asked to conduct an anti-drug assembly sponsored by the FCA (Fellowship of Christian Athletes) at that school. God really blessed what I was trying to accomplish, because when I met with a few of the principals and guidance counselors, they remembered who I was. They said that I was welcome on that campus anytime.

Luckily, within a two-mile radius of the school, there were three incredible churches. I quickly developed relationships with the student ministers from these churches. We came up with a plan to establish monthly rallies where we combined all our students for one big event. This really worked great. It attracted lots of students who normally would never attend church. God was opening doors left and right for ministry opportunities in that area and on the campus of that high school.

I started a Thursday Bible study after school, and the response was incredible! Students would simply walk across the street from the campus and pile into our church for fellowship and study. Students were learning about Jesus and coming to know Him as their Savior and Lord. It was awesome!

OK, I know you've all been members of a group or club at one time or another—and usually there is ONE individual who stands out head and shoulders above the rest. You know the one I'm talking about—the one who always goes the extra mile—the individual who seeks to help other people no matter what the cost, without expecting any glory for his or her actions. If you are a student minister reading this, you know what a true blessing it is to have a student in your group who tries to reach his or her peers in order to make an impact for the Kingdom of God. Well, I had a student like that in my youth group. Not only was this young man mature beyond his years, he was also touched by the hand of God. He certainly broke the standard mold of a preacher's kid. Yes, that's right—Jonathan was my pastor's son.

Jonathan was an amazing young man. He had a passion for Jesus and a heart to reach his campus for Christ. In addition to these qualities, he also possessed natural athletic abilities in a variety of sports. He reminded me of myself at the age of sixteen, except for one thing. I chose to run from God's will in my life, and I succumbed to various temptations. But Jonathan knew at this early age that he was called to the ministry and was already preparing himself! Jonathan had an incredible gift to take Biblical passages and relate them to real-life circumstances, and he used that gift to reach young people for Christ. OK, I know you've heard the old saying, "What goes around comes around." Well, boy, did it ever!

Let me set the stage. It was Friday evening, just after school let out, and there I sat in my office (what the students in our church commonly referred to as the basement) reading Scripture and studying for Sunday school. All of a sudden I heard the thunder of footsteps coming down the stairs toward my office. Before I could raise my eyes, there was Jonathan, standing in front of me with a look on his face that I knew all too well. He pulled up a chair to sit down and let out a long, deep breath. I could sense his frustration. Trying to keep cool and maintain my composure, I glanced up from my work with a purposeful look of unconcern. Then I asked, "What's up, Jonathan? I can tell something is on your mind." At the same time I was thinking, *Uh-oh. Here it comes.* Then he spoke.

"Todd," he said, "I'm really struggling with some issues at school. Some of my friends are really pressing the issue of having sex. You know I've been going out with Ashley for over six months now, and my buddies are constantly asking me if we've 'done' anything, because a lot of them already have. Although Ashley and I haven't done anything, I feel like I need to know how to respond to their questions and comments. I know in my heart that, even though the temptations are there, Ashley and I have promised each other to focus on God's will in our relationship. I know that Ashley and I are able to resist those temptations because of our walk with Jesus. But how do I explain to my friends and reach them on a level that will make sense when they're NOT walking with God?"

I quickly interrupted, thinking I could just stop the whole discussion and solve this problem with a few Scriptures that had been handed down to me. So, based on wisdom from years before, I quickly opened my Bible and began to share the following verses:

1 Corinthians 10:13—*No temptation has seized you except what is common to man. And God is faithful; he will not let you be tempted beyond what you can bear. But when you are tempted, he will also provide a way out so that you can stand up under it.*

1 Corinthians 6:18–20—*Flee from sexual immorality. All other sins a man commits are outside his body, but he who sins sexually sins against his own body. [19]Do you not know that your body is a temple of the Holy Spirit, who is in you, whom you have received from God? You are not your own; [20]you were bought at a price. Therefore honor God with your body.*

Ephesians 5:3—*But among you there must not be even a hint of sexual immorality, or of any kind of impurity, or of greed, because these are improper for God's holy people.*

1 Corinthians 6:13—*The body is not meant for sexual immorality, but for the Lord, and the Lord for the body.*

1 Thessalonians 4:3–5—*It is God's will that you should be sanctified: that you should avoid sexual immorality; 4that each of you should learn to control his own body in a way that is holy and honorable, 5not in passionate lust like the heathen, who do not know God . . .*

Matthew 5:28—*"But I tell you that anyone who looks at a woman lustfully has already committed adultery with her in his heart."*

Before I could finish reading the Scriptures, Jonathan stopped me and said, "Come on, Todd, I've already read all of those! Have you forgotten? I AM the preacher's son! I've already researched this subject. That's why I'm coming to you. I've already shared those Scriptures with my friends. I'm not dealing with idiots—these guys are smart! With every verse I throw at them, they can argue every point. For example, here's the stuff they're coming up with:"

- ○ Come on, man. I'm not being immoral.
- ○ I really love this girl. She means everything to me.
- ○ It's not like I want to commit some kind of sexual crime.
- ○ I'm not doing anything unnatural.
- ○ I just want her to know how much I really love her.
- ○ I honestly think this is the girl I might marry one day.

- ○ I'm not lusting after her. I really care about her.
- ○ I'm not committing adultery. Neither one of us is married.
- ○ PLEASE, I want a verse that literally hits me over the head with a two-by-four.
- ○ Why can't there be a chapter in the Bible that specifically tells you what you can and can't do when you're dating?
- ○ Just show me in the Bible where it says word for word, DO NOT HAVE SEX BEFORE YOU'RE MARRIED!

Man, this sounded all too familiar! Jonathan continued, "PLEASE, help me come up with something that will make sense to them. I need something that answers the question, 'How Far Is Too Far?' without leaving any room for doubt. I mean, I know that it all boils down to a person's spiritual walk and how deep his or her commitment is to follow Jesus Christ. But isn't there an answer that makes perfect sense even when your walk with God isn't perfect?"

> **But isn't there an answer that makes perfect sense even when your walk with God isn't perfect?"**

So there it was. The proverbial question hung in the air. You know, the question that every student minister loves, longs for, and prays earnestly to hear on a daily basis. Yeah, right! (Did I forget my dental appointment today? Where's the nitrous? What—a root canal?)

There I was, completely and utterly dumbfounded. For once in my life, I could not overcome my own "deer in the headlights" look with my usual gift of gab. An uneasy silence filled the room. But now the tables had turned! I had NOTHING to say to Jonathan. I mean—I couldn't use the solution Don had used on me years before. Remember? Where is your spiritual walk—The Five Minute Challenge? Up to this point in my ministry, Jonathan had one of the best spiritual walks of anyone I knew. What was I to do?

I did the only thing I could—I RAN! (Just kidding.) Seriously, I looked Jonathan right in the face and said, "I DON'T KNOW." But I quickly recovered and stated, "Give me one week, and I promise that I will devote every moment of my free time to finding THE answer to your question." I also challenged Jonathan to do the same.

Then we prayed and asked God to reveal an answer that made perfect sense. Not only did we pray for that, but we also prayed that the answer would be so in-your-face that it left no room for debate. We even went a step further and asked God to reveal His answer on this subject, through Scripture, without using the standard verses that churches have always leaned on. We specifically prayed that God would show us the answer without using any of the following words: sexual immorality, fornication, impurity, lust, or adultery. Simply stated, we literally wanted God to hit us over the head with a two-by-four and leave no room for doubt that it was HIS answer and not ours. At this point, we got up off our knees, gave each other a big bear hug, and the week began.

As that week progressed, I became increasingly frustrated. By Wednesday, I was actually getting angry with God for not giving me the answer for which I had prayed so earnestly. So, I threw my hands up in the air and declared, "Forget it!" I walked out of my office, got into my car, and headed off to clear my head—nothing like some good old rock-n-roll to forget about your cares. You do remember my favorite bands, right?

After driving around for a couple of hours, I returned to my office to prepare for Wednesday night Bible study. I opened my Bible to the book of Matthew and proceeded to read Scripture I had probably read a hundred times before. All of a sudden, I was hit over the head with a two-by-four—and it hit me hard! One verse led to another and then another. This was so cool! It was exactly what Jonathan and I had prayed for. It had been there all along in His Word, but I had never heard these verses used for this subject matter. I couldn't wait to share with Jonathan what God had revealed!

After showing Jonathan what I had learned, I could visibly see the burden being lifted from his shoulders. His eyes lit up and he simply said, "That's IT!" Since that day, God has opened doors for me to speak and share this message with many churches and student ministers. Now, I would like to share it with you.

Luke 14:26—*"If anyone comes to me and does not hate his father and mother, his wife and children, his brothers and sisters—yes, even his own life—he cannot be my disciple."*

Because when we take Christ in, when we not only sample what He has to offer, but literally consume His word and make it part of us, He changes us. He becomes part of us and we become part of Him and part of the spiritual body that makes up the church.

The Paradigm Shift

all right, so here we are—the moment you've been waiting for. I highly caution you NOT to read any further unless you're willing to experience a paradigm shift (a change from one way of thinking to another). For most of us, no matter what our age, on some level have asked the question, "How Far Is Too Far?" Oh, come on. Let's get honest. We've all asked that question. Let me share a little story with you.

While writing this book, I was teaching a ninth-grade boys' Sunday school class at the church I attend. One Sunday after church, some of the guys invited me to go to a local mall in the Dallas/Fort Worth area just to hang out and get a bite to eat. While sitting at the table and enjoying some of our favorite junk food, one of the guys asked my opinion on dating. The conversation was based on a Bible study they had attended a few days earlier. The topic was on dating. But instead of answering their questions concerning premarital relationships, they still seemed slightly dazed and confused. As I listened to each of the students chime in one by one, recalling the Bible study, I started thinking, *This information is the same stuff I heard when I was their age. Nothing's changed.* I was laughing inside as they struggled to explain their different points of view about dating and relationships. You know, like: Should Christians even date? Are you allowed to hold hands? Are you allowed to kiss? Are you allowed to touch? What are you allowed to do?

One of the young men, who has a great relationship with Jesus, actually said, "I believe that you should date as many people as possible, because if you don't, then how will you know when the right person comes along?" Another young man spoke up and immediately said, "You're crazy, dude. That's not what we're supposed to do. God's got one person in mind for us, and you'll just know when that person comes along."

As they shared their beliefs, I couldn't help but think, "God did NOT mean for his children to be confused about this subject." I am convinced that Satan can and does use the church to twist the intended meaning of its message to confuse young adults and singles on where they should draw the line on premarital sex and physical intimacy. I believe that the more young adults and singles debate or argue about this subject, the more tolerant they become of what society says is acceptable. Inevitably, somebody always stakes the claim, "If you really love someone, and you believe in your heart that he or she is the person you intend to spend the rest of your life with, then how can premarital sex be wrong when it seems so right?"

Sitting right there in the mall food court, in the middle of all this confusion, I realized it was the perfect opportunity to test what God had shown me about physical intimacy and dating. At that point, I finally spoke up and said, "All right, y'all want my opinion?" They immediately said, "That's why we brought it up!"

I started by saying, "OK, before I start, I want you to understand that what you're about to hear will change your life. Because what I'm going to share with you will make things so crystal clear, that you will never have to argue or debate on this subject again. So with that said, if you still want to stay confused, get up and walk away now." No one moved.

Now, keep in mind what I was up against. We were not in a church setting. We were in the middle of one of the busiest malls in the entire country. And, truth be told, young men do not go to the mall to shop—not for clothes, anyway. While walking through the mall, and even when we sat down to eat, the guys had plenty of "eye candy" to distract them. But once I started to speak, I could not believe how tuned in these young men were. It was as if I were about to tell them how they could win a million dollars. I could tell this was important to them.

By the time I was through sharing my thoughts and convictions on the subject matter at hand, the same student who stated, "You should date as many people as possible," leaned across the table and said, without blinking, "Dude. That's it! You've just made my life so much easier." Another said, "Wow. That leaves no room for debate. It's impossible to argue with that." And finally, one of the guys actually said, "You should write a book and share this with everyone." I laughed a little and said, "I'm working on it."

Have I strung you out long enough? All right already—here we go.

Remember all those verses I talked about in Chapter 1 and mentioned again in Chapter 5—the ones I argued with Don until I was blue in the face? You know, the Scriptures that are so powerful, that alone they could stomp out any argument or debate concerning premarital sex or physical intimacy! The verses that, as a result of living in the gray area, I had the audacity to believe I was smart enough to take from the Word of God (the Creator of the Universe) and to distort His infallible Truth into whatever I wanted it to mean for my particular situation and satisfaction. Sound familiar? It was during that time I declared, **"I want an answer that makes perfect sense, even when my 'walk' with God isn't perfect"**—therefore leaving no gray area.

So, assuming that most of us do NOT have a perfect walk with God, and that we probably have some gray area in our lives, I would like to attack the subject of premarital sex and physical intimacy from a completely different angle—one you haven't thought of before. So, let's try a new approach.

Christ said the following:

> **Matthew 18:3**—*"I tell you the truth, unless you change and become like little children, you will never enter the kingdom of heaven."*

The Scripture also reads:

> **1 Corinthians 14:33a**—*God is not a God of confusion but of peace.*

Based on that, I believe Christ is NOT in the business of leaving His children in a state of confusion concerning any subject—especially one that has plagued young adults for so many years. Any time a group of believers disputes what the Word of God says on a particular subject, it is NOT of God. It is of Satan.

With that said, I have to ask you a fundamental question. **Do you believe that the blood of Christ truly has the power to cleanse you from all unrighteousness?** If you answered "yes" to this question, then stop what you're doing, turn off any distractions, and ask the Lord the following:

○ Please open my mind to a new ideology based on Your Scripture.

○ Please soften my heart and allow Your spirit to move and convict me as You see fit.

○ Please purify and cleanse my environment from anything that could hinder me from comprehending what I'm about to read.

○ Please, based on Your will, let me take from this book what You would have me take and apply to my life.

OK, let me introduce you to some Scriptures that the Lord revealed to me while taking that initial challenge with Jonathan. The following verses are the crux of the message God related to me. I had probably read these Scriptures a hundred times before God allowed me to draw from them a message about physical intimacy and dating. I hope that, by the time we're done, the Lord will have hit you with a Holy two-by-four just like he hit me. Keep in mind that these Scriptures appear to have nothing to say about sexual immorality, promiscuity, lust, etc. But for me, they hold the answer to the question, "How Far Is Too Far?" So here they are:

Matthew 12:46–50—*While Jesus was still talking to the crowd, his mother and brothers stood outside, wanting to speak to him. [47]Someone told him, "Your mother and brothers are standing outside, wanting to speak to you." [48]He replied to him, "Who is my mother, and who are my brothers?" [49]Pointing to his disciples, he said, "Here are my* mother and my brothers. [50]For whoever does the will of my Father in heaven is my brother and sister and mother."

Mark 3:31–35—Then Jesus' mother and brothers arrived. Standing outside, they sent someone in to call him. [32]A crowd was sitting around him, and they told him, "Your mother and brothers are outside looking for you." [33]"Who are my mother and my brothers?" he asked. [34]Then he looked at those seated in a circle around him and said, "Here are my mother and my brothers! [35]Whoever does God's will is my brother and sister and mother."

Mark 10:28–30—Peter said to him, "We have left everything to follow you!" [29]"I tell you the truth," Jesus replied, "no one who has left home or brothers or sisters or mother or father or children or fields for me and the gospel [30]will fail to receive a hundred times as much in this present age (homes, brothers, sisters, mothers, children and fields—and with them, persecutions) and in the age to come, eternal life."

Luke 9:59–62—He said to another man, "Follow me." But the man replied, "Lord, first let me go and bury my father." [60]Jesus said to him, "Let the dead bury their own dead, but you go and proclaim the kingdom of God." [61]Still another said, "I will follow you, Lord; but first let me go back and say good-by to my family." [62]Jesus replied, "No one who puts his hand to the plow and looks back is fit for service in the kingdom of God."

Luke 14:26—*"If anyone comes to me and does not hate his father and mother, his wife and children, his brothers and sisters—yes, even his own life—he cannot be my disciple."*

Notice any recurring themes? First, let me address something. Christ did not mean that He wants us to hate our families. Nor does He want us to abandon our mothers, fathers, sisters, and brothers. Allow me to share with you my thoughts on the verses you just read. Please understand that God revealed the things I'm about to share through countless hours of prayer and study on this particular subject. I strongly encourage you to read, research, and meditate on these Scriptures as well as the other Scriptures quoted throughout this book, in order to draw your own conclusions based on God's word and not mine.

Simply put, I believe that within these verses, Christ is telling us that there is nothing more important in the world than the relationship you have with Him. Back in the day when Christ spoke these words, immediate family was held as the most sacred of all relationships. In some cases, a person's biological bloodline literally defined who he was and what he would become. There was nothing more important. Jesus takes this idea to a whole new dimension. He's telling us that our biological bloodlines are nothing, even less than nothing, in comparison to the spiritual bloodline of Christ.

He is also telling us that whoever or whatever we give up to follow Him will be returned to us, but with holy multiplication.

In Luke 14:26, the word *hate* was actually the Greek word "miseo" or "misos," which means "hatred, to detest, and to persecute," and extends to the meaning "loveless." It was a complete lack of emotion, which is the "true" opposite of love. Hate was not a word people used carelessly to describe their dislike of certain green vegetables. This was SERIOUS stuff! Think about it. Why would Jesus say you couldn't be His disciple unless you hated your own family? Here's my theory: God doesn't want anything in your life to get in the way of what He has planned for you, not even your biological family. Jesus wants to be IT in your life. So when He calls, you'll answer and follow no matter what the cost! He is also telling us that whomever or whatever we give up to follow Him will be returned to us, but with holy multiplication.

I guarantee there are some of you reading this right now who understand what I mean by holy multiplication. Just take a look at your life, or maybe the life of someone close to you, and examine the key people or relationships that have developed as a result of knowing Christ personally. For some of you, He has already placed great Christian people in your life who fill the role of a father or mother when you don't have one at home. For others, God has provided great Christian friends with whom you have built relationships far stronger than relationships with your own brothers and sisters. Others of you have had to give up relationships with biological families to follow Christ. In return, you have gained a family of spiritual fathers, mothers, brothers, and sisters. All this has been made possible through the blood of Jesus.

Check out the following Scripture:

> **John 6:53–56**—*Jesus said to them, "I tell you the truth, unless you eat the flesh of the Son of Man and drink his blood, you have no life in you. 54Whoever eats my flesh and drinks my blood has eternal life, and I will raise him up at the last day. 55For my flesh is real food and my blood is real drink. 56Whoever eats my flesh and drinks my blood remains in me, and I in him."*

OK, let's look at this one. What is Jesus really saying here? I believe He's asking us to jump in with both feet, dive in head first, and "Just do it." (Is that copyrighted?) Because when we take Christ in, when we not only sample what He has to offer, but literally consume His word and make it part of us, He changes us. He becomes part of us and we become part of Him and part of the spiritual body that makes up the church.

Let's read another verse:

> **1 Corinthians 12:12–14**—*The body is a unit, though it is made up of many parts; and though all its parts are many, they form one body. So it is with Christ. 13For we*

were all baptized by one Spirit into one body—whether Jews or Greeks, whether slaves or free—and we were all given the one Spirit to drink. [14]Now the body is not made up of one part but many.

Let's break that down real quick. Here's the best explanation I can come up with:

All believers are baptized by one Holy Spirit into one body of believers—the church. When a person becomes a Christian, the Holy Spirit takes up residence, and he or she is born into God's family. "We were all given the one Spirit to drink" means that the same Holy Spirit completely fills our innermost beings.

All right. At this point, I've got to ask you one more question. Based on what you've been reading, **"Do you believe that the blood of Christ, the Spiritual DNA that binds us to His body, is more powerful than the biological blood that runs through our veins?"**

Think about it for a moment. After reading the previously quoted Scriptures, it shouldn't take you long to come up with a resounding "YES!"

Good—I'm glad we're on the same page. But you're probably still wondering what any of this has to do with dating, physical intimacy, or premarital relationships. If you've made it this far, the big payoff is on the next few pages. But before you move on, be warned . . . once you read the next chapter, you'll have no excuse for not knowing the answer to the question, "How Far Is Too Far?"

For some of you, I bet you already know where this is heading.

Ultimately, our biological DNA binds us to our own mortality, but our Spiritual DNA binds us to each other and to an eternity with Christ.

Fasten Your Seatbelts

I hope you've come to the conclusion that as believers in Christ you are also part of Christ's body. At the end of the last chapter, I introduced a new term: "Spiritual DNA." The point here is that we are bound in one accord by a sacred strain, something that cannot be seen under a microscope—the very blood of Christ. That blood (our Spiritual DNA) is the purest bond the world has known, and will ever know. There are no mutations, diseases, or variations. It is unchanging as God is unchanging, perfect as He is perfect, and holy as He is holy. Throughout human history, slight changes in genetics (gene pools) have resulted in horrible disabilities and imperfections, but the blood of Christ has never changed. Ultimately, our biological DNA binds us to our own mortality, but our Spiritual DNA binds us to each other and to an eternity with Christ.

With that said, I think we can all agree that, as brothers and sisters linked by Christ's blood, it is our obligation to keep that most holy bond free from contamination. What one part of your body does affects the rest of your body, just as your individual actions can either bring shame or honor to your entire family. The following Scripture says it best:

I Corinthians 12:26—*If one part suffers, every part suffers with it; if one part is honored, every part rejoices with it.*

Look at one more passage of Scripture:

1 Corinthians 6:19–20—*Do you not know that your body is a temple of the Holy Spirit, who is in you, whom you have received from God? You are not your own; ²⁰you were bought at a price. Therefore honor God with your body.*

Did you get that? We were bought and paid for by the blood of Christ who suffered on a cross. Our bodies are the temples of the Holy Spirit! Do you really want to be responsible for defiling His temple? We are part of His body! We are bound to Jesus Christ by the precious blood that was spilled out on Calvary. He is our Savior—our Father—our Daddy! We are part of His Family! We are bound together by that perfect strain of "Spiritual DNA" that creates our sacred bond of brotherhood and sisterhood.

At the end of the last chapter, I left you with this question: "What does any of this have to do with dating, physical intimacy, or premarital relationships?" That question can best be addressed by finally answering the question on the cover of this book . . .

> **What you wouldn't DO physically with
> your own biological brother or sister,
> DON'T even THINK about doing with your
> Spiritual brother or sister in Christ.**

There you have it—the answer to the age-old question,
"How Far Is Too Far?" Think about that for a moment.
Here's a much deeper theory to contemplate. You might
want to fasten your seatbelts for this . . .

SPIRITUAL INCEST

Guys, Girls, Young Men, and Young Ladies—hear me
well. This is serious stuff! The Scripture reads:

> **1 Corinthians 6:18**—*Flee from sexual immorality. All
> other sins a man commits are outside his body, but he
> who sins sexually sins against his own body.*

Think about it—sexual sins are the only sins you can commit against your body which require involving someone else
in order for that sin to happen. Don't go there! This is your
brother or sister in Christ we're talking about.

Now, depending on the strength of your spiritual walk with
Christ, some of you may be devising a plan to go around this
impenetrable mountain of biblical truth. You may already be

thinking, *What if I date a non-Christian? Then he or she is not my brother or sister in Christ. No spiritual incest there.* WRONG! We are ALL created in the image of God. Do you really want to risk causing one of God's precious creations to stumble and fall into sin? Just because a person has not accepted Jesus Christ as his or her Savior, doesn't give you the right to use that person for your own physical desires. If anything, you should put forth your best Christ-like example so as not to destroy your witness with non-believers. Not to mention, what you do still affects the body of believers, regardless of whom you do it with. And to take it a step further, read the following Scripture:

2 Corinthians 6:14–18—*Do not be yoked together with unbelievers. For what do righteousness and wickedness have in common? Or what fellowship can light have with darkness? 15What harmony is there between Christ and Belial? What does a believer have in common with an unbeliever? 16What agreement is there between the temple of God and idols? For we are the temple of the living God. As God has said: "I will live with them and walk among them, and I will be their God, and they will be my people." 17"Therefore come out from them and be separate, says the Lord. Touch no unclean thing, and I will receive you." 18"I will be a Father to you, and you will be my sons and daughters, says the Lord Almighty."*

THERE IS NO ARGUING WITH THE WORD OF GOD!

Well, that kind of says it all. Once again, our Father addresses us as sons and daughters, therefore as brothers and sisters. Just in case you still don't catch on, please be on the lookout for my next book, *Christianity for Dummies*. That's a joke, but I hope you get the point. There is NO arguing with the Word of God.

Anyway, the idea of being "equally yoked" is vital to maintaining a consistent walk with Christ. And for those of you still attempting to win souls for the Lord through "missionary dating," just remember this—it is much easier for non-Christians to pull you down than it is for you to pull them up.

At this point, some of you have come to the conclusion—if we are all brothers and sisters in Christ, does that mean I CAN NEVER HAVE SEX?

Relax. Calm down. It's going to be all right; just keep reading.

The spiritual blood that binds us together prohibits physical intimacy because we are all brothers and sisters in Christ.

The Dilemma and the Solution

There are no contradictions with God. He is perfect. Let me assure you that God thinks sex is great. He created it! So, I'll try to ease your fears the best way I know how—with the Word of God.

Here's the dilemma (although it's really not one if you just stick with me). The spiritual blood that binds us together prohibits physical intimacy because we are all brothers and sisters in Christ. But what if I told you there is a solution that can supercede those sacred ties? Would that lift your spirits?

Take a look at the following verses. I think you'll figure this one out on your own.

> **Genesis 2:22–24**—*Then the LORD God made a woman from the rib he had taken out of the man, and he brought her to the man. [23]The man said, "This is now bone of my bones and flesh of my flesh; she shall be called 'woman,' for she was taken out of man." [24]For this reason a man will leave his father and mother and be united to his wife, and they will become one flesh.*

Matthew 19:4–6—*"Haven't you read," he replied, "that at the beginning the Creator 'made them male and female,' [5]and said, 'For this reason a man will leave his father and mother and be united to his wife, and the two will become one flesh'? [6]So they are no longer two, but one. Therefore what God has joined together, let man not separate."*

Mark 10:6–8—*"But at the beginning of creation God 'made them male and female.' [7]'For this reason a man will leave his father and mother and be united to his wife, [8]and the two will become one flesh.' So they are no longer two, but one."*

MARRIAGE—that's your solution!

At the very moment you say "I do" and become husband and wife, God no longer sees you as separate (brothers and sisters), but rather as one. Cool, huh?

"Have you forgotten that almost every great man of God in the Bible failed God miserably at first? They only became great AFTER they surrendered ALL to God!"

Dealing with the Past

OK, let's switch gears for a moment. For some of you, the thought of "Spiritual Incest" is not only an abstract idea, but also a very real burden. And it could distract you from what the Lord wants you to discover about purity and forgiveness. You may feel weighed down by guilt. You may think God can't use you because of your past. STOP! Move on—quit dwelling on what you've done! That's exactly what the "evil one" wants you to do. Satan loves the mistakes of your past because they are the only ammunition he has to make you question your self-worth. Your past does not determine your future if you put God in control. The Bible is full of people with sinful pasts, whom God used in mighty ways. Remember what Stephanie told me in Chapter 4:

> Satan loves the mistakes of your past because they are the only ammunition he has to make you question your self-worth.

"Have you forgotten that almost every great man of God in the Bible failed God miserably at first? They only became great AFTER they surrendered ALL to God!"

That applies to you as well. Also keep in mind the very first Bible verse I mentioned in the preface of this book. It reads as follows:

> **1 John 1:9**—*If we confess our sin, He is faithful and just and will forgive us our sin and cleanse us from all unrighteousness.*

Our God is in the business of not only forgiving but also totally forgetting and separating all our sins from us, as the Scripture below tells us.

> **Psalm 103:11–12**—*For as high as the heavens are above the earth, so great is His love for those who fear Him; ^{12}as far as the east is from the west, so far has He removed our transgressions from us.*

God doesn't focus on what you've done in your past. He desires to guide your future and conform it to His perfect will. Just remember HIS will always prevails.

GIRLS, you are LOVED! You can find hope in Jesus and LOVE that far surpasses any love of an earthly father. And NO boy, guy, or man can fulfill your needs like JESUS!

You must love each other enough to do what is best for each other, and that includes remaining pure until marriage. He is your brother until he is your husband.

Just for the Girls

irls, before I turn the next two chapters over to my partner and co-writer, Doug Haley, I want to address something of great concern. I am convinced one of the leading causes of suicide among young women between the ages of fourteen and twenty-five results from the emotions surrounding sexual tension and temptations. There is a great deal of evidence to support this, and I encourage you to do your own research. Bear with me, and see if the following scenario reminds you of anyone you know. Guys, I know you're reading this too, so pay very close attention.

A young girl is neglected by her father (or is raised without a father) and is never told that she is loved. She seeks affection from the first guy who shows her attention. She buys into the lies and manipulating tactics he throws her way because she wants to be accepted and loved. She feels pressured to have sex. The guy is constantly telling her that he loves her and wants to show his love by expressing it physically. She finally submits to his pressuring and has sex for the first time. She continues on this path for several weeks and months. Suddenly, the guy dumps her for another girl, with no explanation. She is completely devastated. She begins to question her self-worth. The guy starts spreading rumors about her (locker-room talk). She wants to be accepted and liked, so she begins dating guy after guy. All the while her self-worth is withering away. She continues to have sex with more and more guys. The gossip continues to spread. She's now labeled a "whore" or a "slut" in the society in which she lives. She ends up pregnant and has no idea what to do. She confronts the guy she thinks is the father, and he wants nothing to do with her. She confides in her "friends" and they advise her to get an abortion. She has an abortion and the emotional roller coaster really begins. She starts the cycle all over, but this time she numbs the pain with alcohol and drugs. Depression is now settling in as her self-worth is dying rapidly. She sees no hope in sight. Thoughts of suicide begin to race through her head. An overdose! A razor to the wrist! Another statistic!

This could have been avoided if just one of those guys had taken the time to love her as a "Sister in Christ." If just one of those guys had shown her the respect she deserved. If just one had said, "Enough is enough! You're a child of God and HE desires much more for your life." If just one had been man enough to introduce her to her real DAD—Jesus Christ!

GIRLS, you are LOVED! You can find hope in Jesus and LOVE that far surpasses any love of an earthly father. Please know that you are LOVED and that you are the treasure of your FATHER'S eyes. And that NO boy, guy, or man can fulfill your needs like JESUS!

With that said, I would like to turn the rest of this chapter and the next one over to Mr. Doug Haley.

———◆▸✕◂◆———

WOW! That was pretty deep! OK, let's get started. When I was asked to write a chapter just for girls, I thought it would be easy. Man, was I wrong! The idea was to come up with three or four must-know things that would make the road of male/female relationships a little easier to navigate. But the more I thought about it and prayed about it, the more I realized this could be a whole book in itself!

So, what did I do? I simply relied on that age-old solution to almost any problem: procrastination. I've been putting it off for months! In fact, if procrastination were an Olympic sport, I'd be wearing the gold! But just as all good things must come to an end, the time has arrived to tackle this project. Pray right now that God will speak to you in the next few pages.

My wife and I teach the college/career Sunday school class at our church. This past weekend we took a bunch of these students, ages seventeen to twenty-six, up to a mountain cabin for a weekend retreat. While there, I posed this question to them: if you had to give advice to a teenage girl regarding GUYS, what would be the three most important things she should know? I knew there was very little chance they could limit their thoughts to just three things, but I threw it out there anyway. Their replies were interesting and very much to the point.

> **Girls, you have simply GOT to stop letting your boyfriend (or lack of one!) define who you are and how you feel about yourself!**

First: Make your relationship with Christ Jesus the #1 priority. Period. No exceptions. This was at the top of the list by unanimous consent. Until that vertical relationship is vital and growing, you are not ready for a boyfriend/dating relationship! You will get shredded. Been there, done that—right? Until you understand how much your Father loves you; until you learn to let Jesus define your true value as a person and fill your deepest needs for love; until you are ready, willing, and able to put no other gods (including that hot guy) before Him—you are a walking recipe for heartache.

Girls, you have simply GOT to stop letting your boyfriend (or lack of one!) define who you are and how you feel about yourself! As a child of the King, you should be defined by what God says about you! And God says you are worth His Son's life. That defines your true worth. You are PRICELESS! No boyfriend, no matter how perfect he may be, can EVER fill that God-shaped hole in your life. If you expect ANY person to meet those needs that only God can meet, you will be hurt over and over again.

Second: Make a list. Sit down, pray, and ask God to help you make a list of characteristics that your perfect lifetime mate would have. If the guy you are thinking about dating doesn't match the list, don't go out with him! Guard your heart. Don't risk falling for ANY guy who does not meet your requirements. NEVER settle for less.

While I was writing this chapter, my oldest son was dating a delightful Christian girl who had quite a list of qualities she wanted in a man. She has given me permission to share her list with you. Some entries are kind of quirky and just for fun. Others are as serious as it gets. Her list follows:

- He must be strong in his Christian faith no matter what comes his way.
- He can't feel intimidated by me.
- He needs to engage in intelligent conversation with me.
- He must be a leader, not a follower.
- He must have a daily walk with Jesus.
- He must not be afraid to share his faith.
- He must be able to laugh at silly things.
- He must always try to have a good time.
- He must respect me—I want to be treated like a lady.
- He must have nice teeth.
- He must like kids and have an awesome time with them.
- He must do small things for me, like sweet notes, flowers, candy, and such.
- He must be dependable. He must do what he says.
- He must be honest.

○ He must be willing to "fess up" when he's done something wrong.

○ He must get along with my parents as well as his.

○ He must understand my goals in life and encourage me toward them.

○ He must be willing to dance with me at any moment and in any place.

○ He must always tell me what he feels.

○ He must have good manners.

○ He must give me affirmation/assurance.

○ He must make simple decisions, such as where to go, whom to invite, etc.

○ He must be willing to pray with me.

○ He must listen to me and never shut me out.

○ He must be the "Spiritual Leader" in our relationship.

> **The single most important thing you need to look for when you are hunting for the perfect guy is the condition of his heart! Is he or is he not a Christian?**

Whew! Quite a list! I'm not saying it should be yours, but I'm simply trying to give you an idea and a starting place. The point is, the world is full of cute guys. You could go to your school or place of work, close your eyes, throw a rock, and hit four or five! But to base your most serious earthly relationship on how a guy LOOKS—how much sense does that make? And how well has that worked for you in the past?

The single most important thing you need to look for when you are hunting for the perfect guy is the condition of his heart! Is he or is he not a Christian? No missionary dating! It just doesn't work. Sure, be his friend. Yes, invite him to church and introduce him to Jesus. But don't let your heart get involved romantically! For any long-term successful relationship to work, you MUST share the same core values, you MUST have a shared commitment to the Lord Jesus Christ, and you must BOTH be growing in your relationship with Him separately before you can hope to grow in your relationship with Him as a couple. This is absolutely essential!

Third: Be up front with each other regarding your commitment not to have sex before marriage. Then do what it takes to make that purity happen! Go out in groups and avoid being alone together. Find something else to do besides cuddling alone on the couch watching TV.

Speaking of which, be selective in what you watch, both on TV and in the theater. Have you ever stopped to think about the influence those images have on your thoughts and values? It is HUGE! Let me put it like this: Would you sit there and watch it with Jesus in the room? If the answer is no, then you need to realize that He IS there. Turn it off, leave the theater, whatever. Are you serious about this purity thing, or just playing games?

Finally: Pray together. If the guy won't or can't pray with you, dump him! Few actions will be as effective in maintaining sexual purity than praying together before and after each date. It centers your minds on God and focuses on the reality of His presence right there with you all night! Conduct yourself all night long with the realization that your Father is right there with you. All night.

A word of caution on this prayer thing: Prayer is intimate behavior. You will seldom feel as close to another person as when you are praying with him. It is an incredibly intimate activity in which you are humbling yourself before your Creator, and each other. Masks come off and shields are put down. And it is surprisingly easy for Satan to twist and pervert that feeling of closeness and turn it into a sexual encounter. Pray together? Yes. But continue to use good judgment regarding time alone together, etc.

While I had all these young minds and hormones together on the mountain, I posed another question to the guys: What is the one thing that girls can do to help YOU maintain a proper relationship with God and with them? All around the room, at the SAME time, came the SAME answer. Ladies, are you listening?

PUT SOME CLOTHES ON AND COVER YOUR BODY!

Guys are programmed for visual stimulation. You may be Crock-Pots, but we are microwave ovens! Low-cut tops, short skirts/shorts, belly tops—I know these are the fashion, but you are making it extremely difficult for guys to keep their thoughts pure! Thoughts lead to actions.

Now, I'm not trying to make excuses for guy's behavior. They are responsible for their actions no matter WHAT you are wearing, and God will hold them accountable. But do you not think that God might hold you accountable as well for providing the "eye candy" that got the ball rolling in that direction? Do you not feel some responsibility to the GUY to help him in this area of weakness?

Keep in mind that this is the answer EVERY guy gave me (from ages seventeen to twenty-six). Ladies, pray for good judgment concerning the choices you make about the clothes you chose to wear. After all, it's the loving thing to do for your brothers in Christ. There will be all the time in the world to flaunt what you've got—for your husband and his eyes only. Jesus told us it would be better to put a big rock around your neck and jump into the ocean than to cause your brother to stumble. He didn't stutter, and your ears didn't flap. Clear as a bell.

To sum it all up, it all goes back to what Jesus said were the two most important things: love God and love others. For a relationship to be successful, you BOTH must love Jesus more than you love each other. Never, ever, put the other person ahead of God in your life. You must love each other enough to do what is best for each other, and that includes remaining pure until marriage. He is your brother until he is your husband.

Until that day, in your dating life you should consider yourself engaged to Jesus!

One last thing! There is an AWESOME book at your local Christian bookstore, entitled *Gift Wrapped by God,* by Dillow and Pintus. In this book you will find a beautiful analogy that may also help you in your commitment to sexual purity. The Bible speaks of Jesus' return as a bridegroom coming for His bride, the church. That would be YOU. Until that day, in your dating life you should consider yourself engaged to Jesus!

Ever have a question about whether your actions are appropriate? Ask yourself, "How would my fiancé feel about what I am doing?" I think the answer will be clear.

YOU ARE LOVED!

Be a growing disciple of Jesus Christ and date ONLY a growing disciple of Jesus Christ. Period. No exceptions. No missionary dating. Guard your heart.

It is your job, your responsibility, to do everything in your power to see that she remains pure and spotless during whatever period of time God entrusts her to your care. Treat her accordingly.

Guys, It's Time to Step Up

OK guys—now it's your turn. I am absolutely certain that you read the previous chapter, "Just For The Girls." Couldn't help yourself, could you? Let's recap, because much of what I said to the girls holds doubly true for you!

First: Make your relationship with Christ Jesus the #1 priority. I know she's hot. I know your heart sings when you're with her. I know she is all you ever dreamed of and more. But if you let her interfere with your love for and time with God, how long do you really think He will put up with that? And what good will you be for her if you are not becoming more and more like Christ each day? Honesty check: Compare the time you are spending with her and the time you are spending with Jesus. Who is your god?

Second: Make a list of your own. It's OK to want a girlfriend you find attractive, but if you are honestly putting that at the top of your list—man, you're in for a rough ride. The "hot" factor is only skin deep, but an ugly heart goes clean to the bone! I have seen some beautiful women who appeared very attractive on the outside, but when they opened their mouths and you caught a glimpse of their heart—well, let's just say that there is no amount of physical beauty that can make up for a rotten heart. What characteristics do you want in a life mate? Know! Invest your heart accordingly.

The single most important thing for a Christian guy is the same as for a Christian girl: **Be a growing disciple of Jesus Christ and date ONLY a growing disciple of Jesus Christ. Period.** No exceptions. No missionary dating. Guard your heart.

Third: Be upfront with each other regarding your commitment not to have sex before marriage.

Finally: Pray together. Make yourself aware that God is right there with you all the time.

Let me tell you a little story. When I was in my early twenties, I attended the state police academy. While there, I met a pretty young girl who was training to be a sheriff's deputy in a nearby county. We got to know each other and started dating after the training was over, even though she lived about 1.5 driving hours from my house. Ahhh—young love!

It so happened that this girl was the daughter of the sheriff in the county where she lived. He was big, strong, mean, and had a reputation as a tough cop—the kind of dad that every guy dreads.

One night the daughter and I were out on a date, and I realized it was getting late. It was getting VERY late; there was no way I could get her home by curfew, and Daddy would be waiting. So there I was, traveling about ninety miles an hour down the interstate, trying to roll the clock backwards, and I blew right by a state trooper!

A quick glance in the rearview mirror told me that I was about to meet one of the state's finest law officers, as his blue lights strobed in the distance. I pulled over to the side of the road, put my own blue light on the dashboard, and hoped he would extend a bit of professional courtesy to a fellow officer from out of town. Hey, it never hurts to try, right?

The trooper pulled right in behind me and very cautiously went through a full-blown felony stop—put your hands where I can see them, etc. When he finally got to my window and asked for some ID, I showed him my badge, introduced him to the sheriff's daughter, and said something like, my name is Doug Haley, and I work for So-and-So County. This is Sheriff Such-and-Such's daughter, and I'm supposed to have her home by 1:00 a.m. Obviously, I'm not going to make it, but I need to get her there as soon as possible.

Luckily, the trooper knew the sheriff and saw the predicament I was in! He simply said, "Well, just sit here for a couple of minutes, then slow down! I've been getting calls up and down the highway from truckers you've been scaring to death! Be careful, and get her home in one piece—and good luck with her dad!"

I got her home. And her dad didn't kill me. But he sure was a scary guy. No way in the world I wanted to have that father on my case about how I was treating his daughter.

Whose daughter is riding in YOUR car? I'll tell you Whose! His name is Jehovah God, and when He spoke, the universe came into existence! He loves that girl more than you ever will—she is His princess, His precious jewel, and the apple of His eye. He sacrificed His Son on a brutal, bloody, Roman cross to purchase her freedom from sin—and she is betrothed to His Son, Jesus Christ!

And this Dad is where? Sitting in the car with you! Kind of puts an interesting light on it, doesn't it? If you lock into the reality of what I just said, it should scare you to death! Pray together, and remember the story.

Just a few more things, guys. I asked the girls on the retreat: What one thing do you need the guys to do to help you remain sexually pure? Here was their answer:

Watch What You Say!

Guys understand very little about what makes a girl tick, but they've figured out one or two things along the way. One of those things is that a girl wants to feel loved. In today's society, so many girls are growing up as emotional cripples because they lack a father in their lives. They are so desperate to find that love, acceptance, and affirmation that the father SHOULD have provided, that they will give themselves to just about any guy who comes along with a smooth line and a reasonable offer.

Guys have learned to push those buttons to manipulate a girl's feelings and emotions. Guys have learned that certain words, phrases, and touches will cause a girl to melt. And the quickest route to a sexual conquest is through the empty phrase, "I love you." Far too many lonely girls will exchange sex for love. And far too many guys have learned to trade that "love" for sex.

Let me be brutally honest here. Are you listening? The truth: If you have sex with a girl before you're married to her, you do not love her at all! Love wants the highest good for the other person. Love puts the other person's well-being ahead of your own. Love is not selfish; it is NOT focused on personal sexual gratification. Love does not use someone in ANY way for personal gain. What you have is runaway hormones and a bad case of lust. Stop kidding yourself and lying to her—it ain't love.

> **It is NOT up to the girl to say NO! It is up to YOU to see that the two of you never get in the situation where she has to say it!**

It's time to step up, guys, and take control of this thing. You are called by God to be the spiritual LEADER in relationships. It is NOT up to the girl to say NO! It is up to YOU to see that the two of you never get in the situation where she has to say it! And YOU will be held accountable before God for that position of leadership.

Take a look at the following:

> **Ephesians 5:23, 25–26**—*For the husband is the head of the wife as Christ is the head of the church . . . ²⁵Husbands, love your wives, just as Christ loved the church and gave himself up for her ²⁶to make her holy, cleansing her by the washing with water through the word.*

You must love girls as Christ loved the church. He gave His life for it. Christ did this so He could set the church apart for Himself. He made it clean, *"By the washing with water through the word."*

Did you get it? As a husband, you will be called to love your wife as Christ loves the church! That is an AWESOME responsibility and challenge. I know you are not married to her yet, but you had better practice that spiritual leadership position NOW! And woe unto you if you put your own selfish sexual desires ahead of her best interests.

We are called to be responsible, loving leaders in our relationships with girls, for THEIR benefit and growth, and for our own as well! Check out the following:

1 Peter 3:7—*Husbands in the same way be considerate as you live with your wives, and treat them with respect as the weaker partner and as heirs with you of the gracious gift of life, so that nothing will hinder your prayers.*

Remember, both husband and wife are to share together the gift of life that lasts forever. **If this is not done, you will find it hard to pray.**

WHOA!! Stop the bus! Did you see that? Failure to understand and RESPECT will put a cork in your bottle of prayer! It doesn't get any more serious than that.

Step up. Take the responsibility to initiate a praying relationship if you choose to date. Take the responsibility of making sure you are not alone together. Take the responsibility to lovingly tell her if her clothing is causing you to stumble. Take the responsibility, the leadership role, of growing in YOUR relationship with Christ and encouraging her to do the same. Practice loving this girl like Christ loves the church. Ponder what it means to lay down your life, your desires, for the good of this other person.

> It is your job, your responsibility, to do everything in your power to see that she remains pure and spotless during whatever period of time God entrusts her to your care.

105

Stop playing with words, stop playing games, and start allowing God to truly love her THROUGH you.

Always remember, and never forget, that she is her Father's daughter. Until she becomes your wife, she is your SISTER in Christ. And she is the fiancée of the Lord Jesus Christ. It is your job, your responsibility, to do everything in your power to see that she remains pure and spotless during whatever period of time God entrusts her to your care. Treat her accordingly.

You have countless opportunities to say "NO." And God always provides a way out.

A Way Out

Man, the last two chapters were awesome! Doug, I can't thank you enough for sharing what was on your heart—it certainly got my attention.

Now, there are a few loose ends to tie up. But first of all, I'd like to get something out of the way by addressing one of the lamest excuses I've ever heard for giving in to sexual temptation. It's the excuse that young people most often recite whenever they tell me about a sexual slip-up. It can be worded in different ways, but the gist is the same. *It just happened; I didn't have time to think about it; I wasn't thinking straight*, and on, and on, and on.

I don't want to hurt your feelings, but I'll be honest with you. Nothing "just happens." Sexual intimacy is always premeditated—no ifs, ands, or buts about it. Humor me through the following scenario:

- O Boy meets girl (or vice versa)
- O Boy finds girl attractive
- O Boy has lustful thoughts about girl

- Boy dwells on those thoughts (I call this "fueling the fire")
- Boy devises a plan to interact with girl
- Boy and girl go on a date
- Boy and girl experience sexual tension on date
- Boy and girl silently wonder about how the date should end (Should we kiss after that Italian food?)
- Boy and girl decide to kiss
- Kissing leads to "other physical activities"
- Boy and girl are now faced with the question, "How Far Is Too Far?"
- Boy and girl go too far

I know these circumstances seem silly, but I hope you can read between the lines. The fact is, when two people are faced with the decision whether or not to become physically intimate, it can never "just happen." You have to say "YES" every step of the way. You have countless opportunities to say "NO." And God always provides a way out. Read the following verse and commit it to memory.

1 Corinthians 10:13—*No temptation has seized you except what is common to man. And God is faithful; He will not let you be tempted beyond what you can bear. But when you are tempted, He will also provide a way out so that you can stand up under it.*

This doesn't work if you enter in to a situation with an "I can handle it" attitude. That will only set you up for fail-

ure. But if you do fail, please don't say, "It just happened."
You and I know better.

Now, I could go on and on with statistics that would
scare you to death concerning premarital sex. You know
what I'm talking about: suicide, depression, sexually
transmitted diseases (STDs), pregnancies before marriage, abortions, date rapes, drug-related sex, and the list
just keeps going on. Most of you who are reading this
book are fully aware of the statistics.

> **Why don't we just stand up and say, not only
> with our mouths but also with our very lives,
> "ENOUGH IS ENOUGH!"**

So here's what I'm trying to figure out: In a world where
information is paramount, where you can find just about
anything with the click of a mouse, where teenagers and
young adults are more intelligent than ever—WHY do
the statistics keep getting worse? Why don't we just stand
up and say, not only with our mouths but also with our
very lives, "ENOUGH IS ENOUGH!"

This book was not designed to "dump" massive amounts
of depressing information on you just to scare you into
sexual abstinence. You don't have to look very hard to
find that on your own. I am completely blown away by
how much information is available at your fingertips.
Check it out. After all, it's your generation and you guys

must do something about your future—and you must do it NOW!

At least one thing is for sure—the answer has been provided to the age-old question, "How Far Is Too Far?" No more excuses. It just doesn't get any clearer than what I have put before you in this book, or I should say, what GOD has put before you in HIS book. I just played a small part in pointing out the obvious.

**Nothing will ever change
until it changes with YOU!**

The Challenge

Bottom line, most of the sexual tension between young adults and singles could be avoided if we just "sold out" for GOD. Most of us struggle with "giving in" because our relationship with Christ is halfhearted! We want "fire insurance," but we're not willing to pay the premiums for the coverage.

I think the reason this generation hasn't risen up and declared, "ENOUGH IS ENOUGH" is because an attitude of "moral relativism" prevails. You may not have heard the term before, but you know what it means. It's everywhere—all that junk about "There is no absolute truth," and "Whatever is right for you is OK as long as it doesn't hurt anyone else." The sad thing is, this generation has bought into that lie—hook, line, and sinker. Think about it—do you look at moral and ethical issues in terms of "black and white" or "wrong or right," or is there always a "maybe" factor? Someone once said, **"You've got to stand for something, or you'll fall for anything."**

For what do you stand, or more importantly, for WHOM?

I am convinced that GOD hates the gray areas in our lives. Christ clearly addresses this very issue in the following Scripture, where He said:

> **Revelation 3:15-16**—*"I know your deeds, that you are neither cold nor hot. I wish you were either one or the other! [16]So, because you are lukewarm—neither hot nor cold—I am about to spit you out of my mouth."*

Do you think Christ is telling us something here? Do you think Christ wants us to take a stand for what's right and wrong and quit straddling the fence? Do you think Christ is telling us that He is disgusted with people who have "gray" in their lives? Do you think Christ wants us to give our ALL for HIM and HIS cause? The answers to these questions contain the solution.

Here it is! Nothing will ever change until it changes with YOU! I truly believe GOD is asking young people all over the world to RISE UP and declare "ENOUGH IS ENOUGH!" I truly believe GOD is calling teenagers, young adults, and singles to take a strong stand and "SELL OUT" instead of "PLAYING CHURCH." I truly believe GOD is calling HIS children to lean on HIM and never back down from biblical truths. I truly believe GOD is calling a generation of young people to step forward, band together, and hold one another accountable as brothers and sisters in Christ. It's time to take back the purity and innocence that Satan has robbed from this generation. ARE YOU READY?

OK. Here is the *How Far Is Too Far?* Challenge. This is a call to action! I believe this "sexual purity" thing needs to go to the next level. I think it's time to go beyond signing commitment cards and wearing rings or bracelets. I believe it takes someone just like you reading this right now to fall on your knees and pray the following:

"I'm tired of being lukewarm! I'm tired of giving in to peer pressure! I'm tired of allowing Satan to manipulate me! I'm tired of watching my brothers and sisters in Christ become statistics! I'm tired of standing on the sidelines and not making a difference! I'm tired of being a 'wimp' when I should be a 'champion' for GOD! I'm tired of my actions hurting the body of Christ! I'm tired of causing my brothers and sisters to stumble! I'm just TIRED!"

BUT . . .

"I'm ready to be on fire for God! I'm ready to say NO when I should say NO! I'm ready to trust God and not care what other people think! I'm ready and willing to give my past and future to GOD and turn my back on Satan and his lies! I'm ready to hold my brothers and sisters accountable for their actions because I love them! I'm ready to get off the sidelines and get in the game! I'm ready to make a difference in the Kingdom of GOD! I'm ready to be a 'champion' for Jesus! I'm ready to stand tall and edify the body of Christ! I'm ready to become a 'true' Spiritual brother and sister. I'm READY!"

If you prayed that prayer, I want to hear from you. Please go to the following Web site:

www.howfaristoofar.com

Click on the "contact us" icon and let me know about your new covenant with GOD. Please do not contact me if you are not serious. This is NOT a game or a contest! Nothing changes unless you pray first and take action second! God isn't looking for any half-hearted commitments. He already has enough of those, and just look where the world is today. If you're serious, I want to know. I want to know if you prayed that prayer so my team of prayer warriors can pray for your strength.

I pray that this book has touched you spiritually, and may God bless you.

Thanks for your support,

What you think may be fun and exciting at the time, could have catastrophic consequences that affect the rest of your life.

Epilogue

This book was written to confront the issue of premarital sex and physical intimacy head-on—without pulling any punches. With that said, the temptations that I struggled with in this book are centered on one thing—sex! This book only scratches the surface of all the idiotic and unbelievably stupid things I participated in as a teenager and young adult. God has spared me from so many heartaches that I couldn't even begin to list them.

The point of this section is to let you know how things turned out for me. Just so you know, I still struggle with the sins of my past. That's the worst thing about sin—the constant struggle with the aftermath. Remember this: Satan will always use your past sins against you when it benefits him the most. That is why you must stay in the Word and stay in constant contact with Jesus Christ. "Pray continually." (1 Thessalonians 5:17) If you follow that simple advice, you will recognize temptations immediately and stop them in their tracks—without committing the actual sin. Just remember: What you think may be fun and exciting at the time, could have catastrophic consequences that affect the rest of your life.

My life drastically changed when I came to the following conclusion: The key to getting over your past is in direct correlation to your belief in the absolute truth based on the Word of God. For instance, do you believe that the following verse is perfectly true, without error, and is without a doubt from the very hand of God?

> **1 John 1:9**—*If we confess our sin, He is faithful and just and will forgive us our sin and cleanse us from all unrighteousness.*

What about this verse?

> **1 Corinthians 10:13**—*No temptation has seized you except what is common to man. And God is faithful; he will not let you be tempted beyond what you can bear. But when you are tempted, he will also provide a way out so that you can stand up under it.*

I believe that our level of belief can and does determine our faith. Our actions are based on our belief. In other words, if we believe the Word of God to be absolutely true and without error, then our actions should reflect that. When we sin against God, we should immediately repent and trust that God actually forgives that particular sin. You see, when we continually dwell and focus our thoughts and energy concerning a particular sin over and over again, by our actions we are telling God that we really do NOT believe that He forgave us! That very lack of belief determines our level of faith at that particular time in our lives. Think about that for a moment—pretty scary, huh?

The point I am trying to make is this: It all boils down to self-forgiveness. In order to totally forgive yourself, you MUST believe wholeheartedly that God means what He says. God is without error! What He says, He does—no ifs, ands, or buts about it!

When I came to that realization in my life, I truly forgave myself for my past. Remember what I said back in Chapter 4:

> "I looked at myself in a whole new light. I looked at myself in the newness of God, clothed not in the filth of my own past, but in the righteousness of Christ! I looked at myself as a new creation of God. I saw myself as someone worthy to serve God—not because of anything I had accomplished, but rather, because of what Jesus had accomplished for me!"

That is what it takes! At that moment my life changed. When I truly forgave myself, my actions reflected my belief in God's infallible truths. I no longer allowed Satan to keep me down; instead, I placed my trust in Jesus Christ and allowed Him to lift me up. HE did and HE still does!

At that pivotal point in my life, I believe the Lord started blessing me beyond my wildest imagination.

God is so awesome! In spite of my past, He introduced me to an amazing woman, who is now my wife! Stacy is an extremely talented and beautiful lady. Can you believe that I married a beauty queen? That's right, my wife is a former Miss Louisiana! What's really cool is that she is far more beautiful now than she was when she wore that crown. But her inner beauty is what continually blows me away. She never ceases to amaze me! She is incredibly talented in so many areas, that I would have to write a separate book to do her justice. I wasn't kidding in the acknowledgement section of the book when I expressed, "I am living proof that you can marry way out of your league."

Not only has God blessed me with an amazing wife, he has granted Stacy and me the ability to support various ministries with our talents and resources. And He continually opens doors for new ministry opportunities.

Currently, the Lord has provided Stacy and me with amazing careers. We are both members of an incredible church in which I am active in the student ministry program. He has blessed me with the challenge of teaching ninth-grade boys' Sunday school. I also work closely with the student minister in developing new opportunities for growth and discipleship training. GOD is great!

Know this: I truly believe I would still be swimming in my past sin if I had not surrendered to God's absolute truth, found in His Scriptures. I believe that Satan's greatest accomplishment is getting a child of God to believe he or she is worthless. Satan does this by keeping us in a guilt-ridden state. If he succeeds at that, we will have no self-worth. I know—I've been there!

Remember this little saying; I'm sure you've heard it before.

GOD does not make junk!

God has a purpose for each and every one of you, no matter what your past. He doesn't make mistakes. Believe that and live it! You are a child of God! So, act like it!

John 8:11b—*And Jesus said, "Neither do I condemn you; go your way. From now on sin no more." (NAS)*

Scripture References

1 John 1:9—*If we confess our sin, He is faithful and just and will forgive us our sin and cleanse us from all unrighteousness.*

I Corinthians 10:13—*No temptation has seized you except what is common to man. And God is faithful; he will not let you be tempted beyond what you can bear. But when you are tempted, he will also provide a way out so that you can stand up under it.*

I Corinthians 6:18–20—*Flee from sexual immorality. All other sins a man commits are outside his body, but he who sins sexually sins against his own body. 19Do you not know that your body is a temple of the Holy Spirit, who is in you, whom you have received from God? You are not your own; 20you were bought at a price. Therefore honor God with your body.*

Ephesians 5:3—*But among you there must not be even a hint of sexual immorality, or of any kind of impurity, or of greed, because these are improper for God's holy people.*

I Corinthians 6:13b—*The body is not meant for sexual immorality, but for the Lord, and the Lord for the body.*

1 Thessalonians 4:3–5—*It is God's will that you should be sanctified: that you should avoid sexual immorality;* *⁴that each of you should learn to control his own body in a way that is holy and honorable,* *⁵not in passionate lust like the heathen, who do not know God . . .*

Matthew 5:28—*"But I tell you that anyone who looks at a woman lustfully has already committed adultery with her in his heart."*

2 Timothy 2:22—*Flee the evil desires of youth, and pursue righteousness, faith, love, and peace, along with those who call on the Lord out of a pure heart.*

Ephesians 6:10–18—*Finally, be strong in the Lord and in his mighty power.* *¹¹Put on the full armor of God so that you can take your stand against the devil's schemes.* *¹²For our struggle is not against flesh and blood, but against the rulers, against the authorities, against the powers of this dark world and against the spiritual forces of evil in the heavenly realms.* *¹³Therefore put on the full armor of God, so that when the day of evil comes, you may be able to stand your ground, and after you have done everything, to stand.* *¹⁴Stand firm then, with the belt of truth buckled around your waist, with the breastplate of righteousness in place,* *¹⁵and with your feet fitted with the readiness that comes from the gospel of peace.* *¹⁶In addition to all this, take up the shield of faith, with which you can extinguish all the flaming arrows of the evil one.* *¹⁷Take the helmet of salvation and the sword of the Spirit, which is the word of*

God. *18And pray in the Spirit on all occasions with all kinds of prayers and requests. With this in mind, be alert and always keep on praying for all the saints.*

2 Corinthians 6:14–18—*Do not be yoked together with unbelievers. For what do righteousness and wickedness have in common? Or what fellowship can light have with darkness? 15What harmony is there between Christ and Belial? What does a believer have in common with an unbeliever? 16What agreement is there between the temple of God and idols? For we are the temple of the living God. As God has said: "I will live with them and walk among them, and I will be their God, and they will be my people." 17"Therefore come out from them and be separate, says the Lord. Touch no unclean thing, and I will receive you." 18"I will be a Father to you, and you will be my sons and daughters, says the Lord Almighty."*

Matthew 18:3—*"I tell you the truth, unless you change and become like little children, you will never enter the kingdom of heaven."*

I Corinthians 14:33 a—*God is not a God of confusion but of peace.*

Matthew 12:46–50—*While Jesus was still talking to the crowd, his mother and brothers stood outside, wanting to speak to him. 47Someone told him, "Your mother and brothers are standing outside, wanting to speak to you." 48He replied to him, "Who is my mother, and who are my brothers?" 49Pointing to his* disciples, he said, "Here are my mother and my brothers. 50For whoever does the will of my Father in heaven is my brother and sister and mother."

Mark 3:31–35—*Then Jesus' mother and brothers arrived. Standing outside, they sent someone in to call him. 32A crowd was sitting around him, and they told him, "Your mother and brothers are outside looking for you." 33"Who are my mother and my brothers?" he asked. 34Then he looked at those seated in a circle around him and said, "Here are my mother and my brothers! 35Whoever does God's will is my brother and sister and mother."*

Mark 10:28–30—*Peter said to him, "We have left everything to follow you!" 29"I tell you the truth," Jesus replied, "no one who has left home or brothers or sisters or mother or father or children or fields for me and the gospel 30will fail to receive a hundred times as much in this present age (homes, brothers, sisters, mothers, children and fields—and with them, persecutions) and in the age to come, eternal life."*

Luke 9:59–62—*He said to another man, "Follow me." But the man replied, "Lord, first let me go and bury my father." 60Jesus said to him, "Let the dead bury their own dead, but you go and proclaim the kingdom of God." 61Still another said, "I will follow you, Lord; but first let me go back and say good-by to my family." 62Jesus replied, "No one who puts his hand to the plow and looks back is fit for service in the kingdom of God."*

Luke 14:26—*"If anyone comes to me and does not hate his father and mother, his wife and children, his brothers and sisters—yes, even his own life—he cannot be my disciple."*

John 6:53–56—*Jesus said to them, "I tell you the truth, unless you eat the flesh of the Son of Man and drink his blood, you have no life in you. 54Whoever eats my flesh and drinks my blood has eternal life, and I will raise him up at the last day. 55For my flesh is real food and my blood is real drink. 56Whoever eats my flesh and drinks my blood remains in me, and I in him."*

I Corinthians 12:12–14—*The body is a unit, though it is made up of many parts; and though all its parts are many, they form one body. So it is with Christ. 13For we were all baptized by one Spirit into one body—whether Jews or Greeks, whether slaves or free—and we were all given the one Spirit to drink. 14Now the body is not made up of one part but many.*

I Corinthians 12:26—*If one part suffers, every part suffers with it; if one part is honored, every part rejoices with it.*

Genesis 2:22–24—*Then the LORD God made a woman from the rib he had taken out of the man, and he brought her to the man. 23The man said, "This is now bone of my bones and flesh of my flesh; she shall be called 'woman,' for she was taken out of man." 24For this reason a man will leave his father and mother and be united to his wife, and they will become one flesh.*

Matthew 19:4–6—*"Haven't you read," he replied, "that at the beginning the Creator 'made them male and female,' ⁵and said, 'For this reason a man will leave his father and mother and be united to his wife, and the two will become one flesh'? ⁶So they are no longer two, but one. Therefore what God has joined together, let man not separate."*

Mark 10:6–8—*"But at the beginning of creation God 'made them male and female.' ⁷'For this reason a man will leave his father and mother and be united to his wife, ⁸and the two will become one flesh.' So they are no longer two, but one."*

Psalm 103:11–12—*For as high as the heavens are above the earth, so great is His love for those who fear Him; ¹²as far as the east is from the west, so far has He removed our transgressions from us.*

Ephesians 5:23, 25–26—*For the husband is the head of the wife as Christ is the head of the church . . . ²⁵Husbands, love your wives, just as Christ loved the church and gave himself up for her ²⁶to make her holy, cleansing her by the washing with water through the word.*

1 Peter 3:7—*Husbands in the same way be considerate as you live with your wives, and treat them with respect as the weaker partner and as heirs with you of the gracious gift of life, so that nothing will hinder your prayers.*

Revelation 3:15–16—*"I know your deeds, that you are neither cold nor hot. I wish you were either one or the other! 16So, because you are lukewarm—neither hot nor cold—I am about to spit you out of my mouth."*

John 8:11b—*And Jesus said, "Neither do I condemn you; go your way. From now on sin no more." (NAS)*

About the Author

Todd Lochner is an ordained minister and former student pastor. He graduated from Louisiana State University. He has been blessed with a successful business career as a result of hard work and determination. Since a young age, he has used that same drive and motivation to spread the Gospel of Christ to young adults and students. He is continually looking for new and creative outlets to use his talents, gifts, resources, and time to impact the lives of young people and introduce them to their Savior and Lord, Jesus Christ. Todd has been fortunate to speak to and perform for tens of thousands of students across the nation. Whether in arenas, concert halls, school assemblies, churches, or small groups, he has been truly blessed to reach people on an extremely personal level.